Microsoft

PowerPoint 2013 Plain & Simple

Nancy Muir

Published with the authorization of Microsoft Corporation by:
O'Reilly Media, Inc.
1005 Gravenstein Highway North
Sebastopol, California 95472

ISBN: 978-0-735-66936-9

1 2 3 4 5 6 7 8 9 QG 8 7 6 5 4 3

Printed and bound in the United States of America.

Microsoft Press books are available through booksellers and distributors worldwide. If you need support related to this book, email Microsoft Press Book Support at *mspinput@microsoft.com*. Please tell us what you think of this book at *http://www.microsoft.com/learning/booksurvey*.

Microsoft and the trademarks listed at *http://www.microsoft.com/about/legal/en/us/IntellectualProperty/Trademarks/EN-US.aspx* are trademarks of the Microsoft group of companies. All other marks are property of their respective owners.

The example companies, organizations, products, domain names, email addresses, logos, people, places, and events depicted herein are fictitious. No association with any real company, organization, product, domain name, email address, logo, person, place, or event is intended or should be inferred.

Acquisitions Editor: Kenyon Brown
Project and Developmental Editor: Laura Krause Sackerman
Production Editor: Holly Bauer
Technical Reviewer: Kristen Merritt
Copyeditor: Bob Russell, Octal Publishing, Inc.
Indexer: Nancy Guenther
Cover Design: Twist Creative • Seattle
Cover Composition: Zyg Group, LLC.
Illustrator: S4 Carlisle Publishing Services

To my colleague, Lisa Bucki, for always being there for me, and to my husband, Earl, for being the perfect partner.

Contents

5   Working with slide masters 65

6   Building a presentation 81

14   Running a presentation 225

15   Printing a presentation 241

16   Sharing a presentation 251

About this book

1

If you are a typical Microsoft PowerPoint user, you lead a hectic life, whether you spend time running from meeting to meeting and conference to conference or driving from the soccer match to a volunteer committee meeting. If your time is valuable, this book is for you. In *Microsoft PowerPoint 2013 Plain & Simple*, you get an easy-to-use reference that helps you get to work immediately. My goals are to help you start building presentations right away and to provide you with information about all sorts of tools and features you can learn about and use over time to create more sophisticated presentations.

This book is based on Microsoft PowerPoint 2013 installed on the Windows 8 operating system, but if you are using Windows 7, you'll find that most of what's described here works just the same. The great new features that PowerPoint 2013 introduces can make your work easier to handle, providing some powerful visual tools for your presentations.

No computerese!

With a presentation deadline staring you in the face, the last thing you want is a lengthy lecture. You need to find out how to accomplish something quickly. This book is structured, task by task, to help you find what you need help with now and to keep you moving.

No task in this book makes you read more than two pages to find an answer to your question. Look up what you need to do in the table of contents or index, follow the steps in the task, and you're done. I don't spend lots of time on elaborate explanations, and you don't need a technical dictionary by your side to understand the steps I describe.

Occasionally, you will encounter a "See Also" element that refers you to a related task simply because some functions overlap each other. You can also find "Tips" here and there that provide helpful advice. Finally, the "Try This" features give you ideas for how to put PowerPoint to use, and "Caution" elements warn you of potential problems. But, the main focus of this book is to keep you on track, providing the information you need, quickly and simply.

Just the essential tasks...

The tasks in this book are organized logically for the types of things that you do in PowerPoint 2013. If you've never built a presentation, you can start at the beginning and work your way through to create your first slide show. However, you don't need to move through the book in order. If you know exactly what you want to accomplish, just find that task and go directly to it!

...and the easiest way to do them

Although PowerPoint 2013 often gives you several ways to get things done, I've tried to suggest the easiest way to get results. The PowerPoint user interface (what you see on the screen) introduced in PowerPoint 2007 and carried on into PowerPoint 2013 has eliminated some methods that you might be used to, such as using menus and toolbars for most tasks, but keyboard shortcuts as well as contextual toolbars and shortcut menus (tools that appear when you perform a certain type of task or right-click a selected item) are still available to address different styles of working. I encourage you to explore the user interface and Help system to find other ways of getting things done after you master the basics.

A quick overview

Although you don't have to read this book from front to back (in fact, you probably won't), it's useful to understand how I've structured it so that you can find your way around.

After you install PowerPoint 2013 (an easy task because the Office installer guides you, step by step), you can begin exploring any of the following sections and their individual tasks.

Sections 2 and 3 introduce you to what's new in PowerPoint 2013 and its user interface, and explain how you move around and work with tools and views in the program.

Sections 4, 5, 6, and 7 start you out building the text portion of a presentation by adding text to individual slides in a graphical environment, by using slide masters (templates by which you can quickly and easily apply global design and text settings to all your slides, handouts, or notes pages), and by entering information into a familiar outline format. You also learn essential information such as how to open and save a presentation either on your computer or your SkyDrive and how to get help. You become acquainted with placeholders on slides, which can contain either text or objects, and begin to understand how you build a presentation, slide by slide, and view the results.

Ribbon   PowerPoint user interface

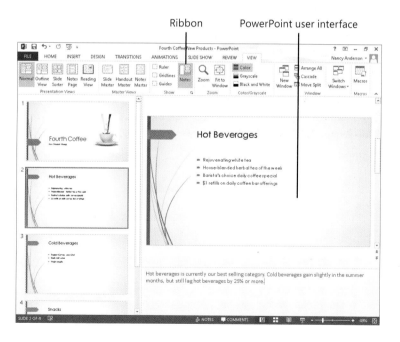

Placeholders   Slide Master Tools

Sections 8, 9, 10, and 11 are where you begin to look at the overall look and feel of slides in various views. You also work with the design aspect of your presentation, using various layouts (different combinations of placeholders and content) and themes and theme variants that contain color and graphical elements. You work with inserting and handling various objects, such as online clip art, WordArt, online videos or video files, and pictures. These sections also provide valuable information on how to format text and other objects in your presentation so that it looks polished and professional.

Sections 12 and 13 take you near to your goal of a final presentation by providing information about slick animations and transitions that you can add to your slides to bring them to life. You also learn about how to set up your show to run as you want it to and how to rehearse, proof, and generally ensure that your presentation is letter perfect.

WordArt gallery

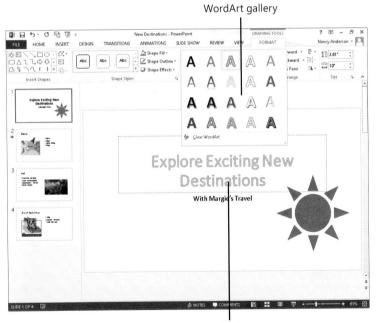

Title slide layout

Symbol indicating an applied transition

Slide Show tools

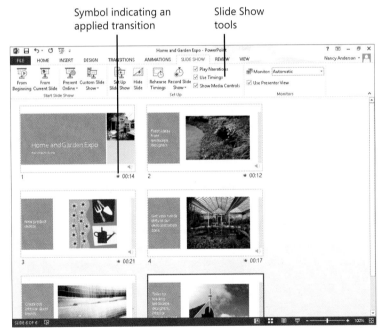

Sections 14, 15, and 16 help you to actually give your presentation to others, either by running it in person, printing hard copies of it, or sharing it via email or the web. This is what all the rest of the work is for, and if you do your job right, you can provide a well-written and well-designed presentation to your audience.

Finally, Section 17 offers information about a few more advanced tools in PowerPoint 2013 that you might want to explore after you master the basics. Among other things, you discover how to create your own presentation templates to save you time, create custom shows from your larger presentation, customize tools on the ribbon tabs, and remove personal information from and digitally sign the presentation.

A slide presentation
displayed full screen

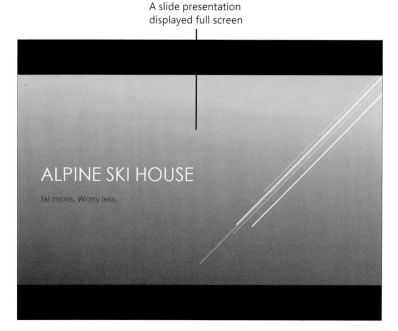

ALPINE SKI HOUSE

Ski more. Worry less.

A few assumptions

When you write a book, you have to first think about your readers. Who are they, what do they already know, and what do they need to know? In writing this book, I've assumed that you are essentially computer literate—you know how to turn your computer on and off, what a mouse is and how to click and double-click items with it, and how to select text or objects. I also assume that you have worked with some kind of software and have at least a passing acquaintance with tool buttons, dialog boxes, and software menus made up of various commands.

Whether you use your computer every day in a high-powered job or spend most of your computer time playing games and writing notes to friends, I assume you have an Internet connection and have been on the Internet. Other than that, this book tries to provide all the steps you need to accomplish the tasks within it in a straightforward way—with plenty of graphics to help you see what I'm talking about.

What's new in PowerPoint 2013?

Like PowerPoint 2007 and 2010, the user interface for Power-Point 2013 continues to revolve around the ribbon, which is a set of tools and controls located at the top of the window. These tools are organized and grouped by function, accessed on tabs that you click. If you only used Office programs prior to Office 2007, you need to become familiar with the ribbon. These tools occasionally offer galleries of choices, and when you move your mouse pointer over these choices, they are previewed on your slides before you apply them. Sometimes, when you work on certain functions, specialized tabs—called *contextual*

tabs—appear; for example, if you select a drawing object, the Drawing Tools|Format contextual tab displays.

PowerPoint 2013 offers improvements to visual elements, including new views, Smart Guides to help you line up shapes and text, variants for getting more variety from themes, enhanced ways to find online clip art to use in your presentation, and the ability to zoom in on part of a slide when you share the presentation in Slide Show view.

Drop-down gallery   Contextual tab

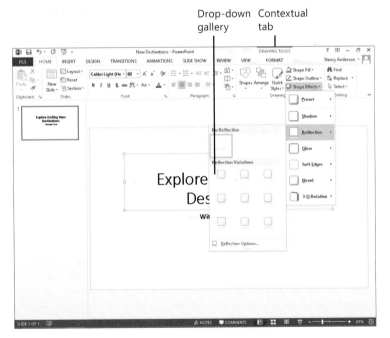

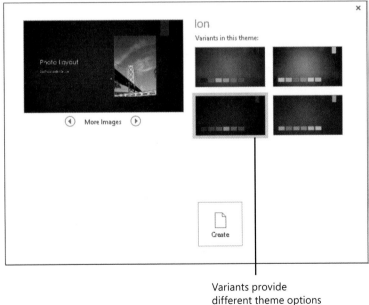

Variants provide different theme options

Finally, PowerPoint 2013 offers more features for sharing presentations with others and broadcasting slide shows on the Internet, including the ability to save a presentation to your SkyDrive folder. I think you'll like what you see after you absorb the changes. PowerPoint 2013 is all about making the tools you work with accessible and obvious.

Options for sharing presentations

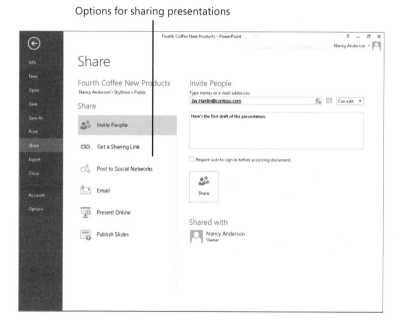

Using a touch-enabled system

PowerPoint 2013 can run on tablets and touchscreen computers. "Understanding touch gestures" in Section 2 provides information about working with touch-enabled devices. For now, here's a brief introduction to touch gestures:

1. **Tap**   Touch and release the screen, much like pressing a keyboard key with your finger. You tap to select buttons and options.

2. **Pinch**   Slide your thumb and index finger together on the screen. You usually do this to zoom out.

3. **Stretch**   Spread your thumb and index finger apart on the screen. You usually do this to usually to zoom in.

4. **Slide**   Tap and hold down on something on the screen, drag to move it, and then release.

5. **Swipe**   A quick finger drag and release, either across or up or down the screen. Swiping is often used for scrolling and selecting.

The final word

This book is designed to make your learning painless, with plenty of visual information to help you pick things up at a glance, along with easy-to-follow steps. My goals are to give you what you need to achieve the task at hand, make tasks easy to find and understand, and help you have fun learning to work with PowerPoint 2013, which is a great design tool that helps you communicate more effectively.

I hope you find the tasks in this book helpful and that you are producing award-winning presentations in no time!

What's new in PowerPoint 2013?

2

Microsoft PowerPoint 2013 features a cleaner, more open screen layout that makes building a presentation easier and more intuitive. Power-Point 2013 sports an easy to use interface that users of PowerPoint 2007 and 2010 will recognize, and it adds even more useful features. This section is where you get your first look at PowerPoint 2013. I'll start by discovering where various tools and settings reside.

The ribbon interface in PowerPoint starts at the left with the File tab, which when clicked (or tapped) displays the Backstage view. There, you can find file-management commands such as New, Open, Save, and Print. Most features are available as buttons on tabs on the ribbon. In some cases, menus or panes are displayed, such as the Research or the ClipArt pane.

Galleries of graphical selections make it possible for you to preview how effects look on your slides or objects before you apply them. There are also several enhanced galleries and formatting options available for you to explore in PowerPoint 2013.

Finally, in this section I'll introduce you to new features, such as Full Screen mode, adding media from online sources to a presentation, and theme variants. You'll also see how you can use SkyDrive.

In this section:

- Launching PowerPoint 2013
- What's where in PowerPoint 2013?
- Understanding touch gestures
- Using the ribbon
- Using new Normal view features
- Using other new view features
- Commenting and using widescreen
- Incorporating online pictures
- Including online video and audio
- Taking advantage of theme variants, Smart Guides, and merge shapes
- Working in the cloud
- Presenting slide shows

Launching PowerPoint 2013

If you're using Windows 8, you will notice right away how easy it is to launch an app on the Start screen. With just a single click, you can be up and working within the PowerPoint 2013 app. When you install PowerPoint 2013 a tile is placed on the Start screen. After you launch PowerPoint from the Start screen, it opens on the Windows desktop. If you're using PowerPoint 2013 in Windows 7, you begin by clicking the Start button in the lower-left corner of the Windows 7 desktop. When you choose All Programs you can navigate to the Microsoft Office 2013 folder and launch the application that you want to use.

Start PowerPoint from the Windows 8 Start screen

1 Scroll through the app tiles on the Start screen.

2 Click the PowerPoint 2013 app tile.

PowerPoint opens on the Windows 8 desktop.

> ➔ **TRY THIS!** If you want to add the PowerPoint 2013 button to the Windows desktop taskbar, select the app tile by swiping down on it or right-clicking it and then click Pin To Taskbar. You can then launch the app by clicking the icon on the desktop taskbar.

> ➔ **TRY THIS!** If you are using PowerPoint on a notebook or desktop computer, you can create a shortcut for launching PowerPoint 2013 on the Windows 8 desktop. To do so, point to the lower-right corner of either the Start screen or the desktop to display the charms. Click the Search charm. Point to the bottom of the screen to display the scroll bar and then scroll right. Right-click the Power-Point 2013 tile and click Open File Location in the commands. In the File Explorer window that appears, ensure that the PowerPoint 2013 shortcut is selected and then press Ctrl+C. Click the desktop and press Ctrl+V. You can then close the File Explorer window.

Start PowerPoint in Windows 7

1 Click the Start button.

The Start menu appears.

2 Click All Programs.

3 Scroll through the programs list and click Microsoft Office 2013.

4 Click PowerPoint 2013.

PowerPoint opens on the Windows 7 desktop.

What's where in PowerPoint 2013?

PowerPoint 2013 uses a central ribbon of tools that you access via various tabs. The tools on the tabs are organized into groups. In addition, you can place your favorite tools on the Quick Access Toolbar, which gathers them in one location and gives you access to functions that aren't offered on the ribbon. Some tools on the ribbon display drop-down galleries of selections or menus with additional choices; others open dialog boxes in which you can set detailed configurations.

Clicking the File tab displays what is known as the *Backstage view*. Here, you can choose from among several common file commands or click the Options command to see a wealth of setting options that you can use to control the way PowerPoint works.

File tab

Ribbon

Contextual tab

Gallery

Group

Dialog Box Launcher

File menu

Options

✓ **TIP** Like Windows 8, PowerPoint 2013 works best when you sign in with a Microsoft Account. If you are already signed in to Windows 8 with a Microsoft Account, that account information will be set up as your primary Office 2013 account. The first time you start PowerPoint, you might be prompted to enter your sign-in information, but after that, sign-in happens automatically.

Understanding touch gestures

The new interface for PowerPoint 2013 has been designed to make it friendlier for tablets and touchscreen computers. The simpler interface leaves room for working with touch gestures that are now recognized in all Office 2013 programs, including the following:

1 Tap, which means to touch and release the screen, much like pressing a keyboard key with your finger. You tap to select buttons and options in PowerPoint.

2 Pinch, which means to slide your thumb and index finger together on the screen, usually to zoom in.

3 Stretch, which means to spread your thumb and index finger apart on the screen, usually to zoom out.

4 Slide, which means to tap and hold down on something on the screen, drag to move it, and then release.

5 Swipe, which means a quick finger drag and release, either across or up or down the screen. Swiping is often used for scrolling and selecting.

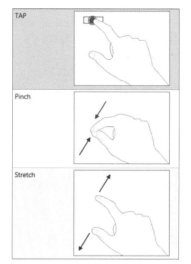

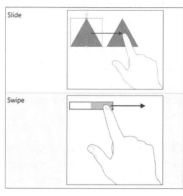

TIP On a tablet or touchscreen computer, tap the Touch Keyboard button on the taskbar to open the On-Screen Keyboard, whose keys you can tap to enter text.

Using the ribbon

The ribbon is your control center in PowerPoint 2013. The default ribbon consists of nine main tabs. There are also contextual tabs that appear now and then when you work with certain types of objects or functions. The Add-Ins tab appears if you install PowerPoint extras or third-party programs that enhance PowerPoint. Each tab presents named groups of commands and options.

Display tabs and panes

1   On the ribbon, click the Review tab.

2   In the Proofing group, click Research to open the Research pane.

3   Click the Close button to close the pane.

(continued on next page)

> **→ TRY THIS!** You can open dialog boxes associated with groups of tools by clicking the dialog box launcher, which is a small arrow that appears at the lower-right corner of many groups on the ribbon. This displays all settings and features related to that category of functions, including some not shown on the ribbon.

> **✓ TIP** If you're using a mouse and you want to find out what a tool on the ribbon does, move the mouse pointer over it. A ScreenTip appears, describing the tool and providing the keyboard shortcut to access it (when one exists). For example, if you place your pointer over the Paste button on the Home tab, you will see the tool name—in this case, Paste—followed by Ctrl+V in parentheses. You can use this keyboard combination to paste an item instead of clicking the button. If you click File and then click Options, you can use the ScreenTip style drop-down list on the General tab of the Options dialog box to control the level of detail in the ScreenTips. Click OK to apply your choice.

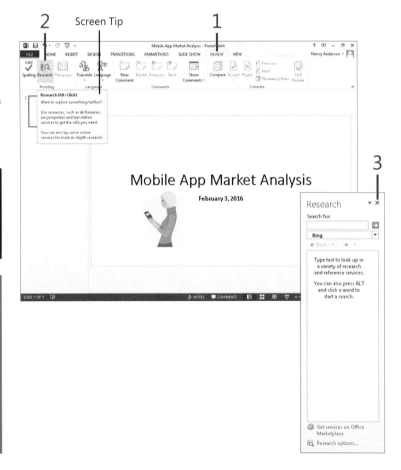

Display tabs and panes (continued)

4 Click the Insert tab.

5 In the Illustrations group, click Shapes and then click an item in the Shapes gallery.

Drag anywhere on the slide to draw the shape.

6 Note that the Drawing Tools|Format tab appears. This is a contextual tab.

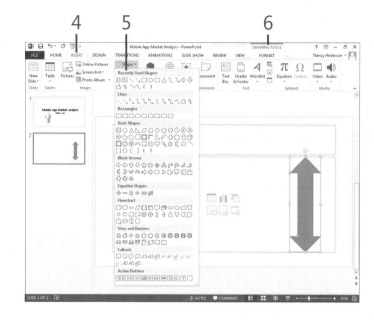

TIP To include add-in programs, click the File tab to display the Backstage view, click Options, and then in the Options dialog box that opens, click the Add-Ins tab. For example, you can include additional presenter tools or presentation notes tools.

TIP Can't find a tool? Some tools, such as AutoCorrect options, are not on the ribbon. In this case, you have to add the tools to the Quick Access Toolbar to perform the function. See the task "Customizing the Quick Access Toolbar" on page 40 for more about how to do this.

Using new Normal view features

Slide show presentations convey information through both visuals and text. That's why it's important to be able to review your presentation in a variety of ways as you work on it. PowerPoint 2013 adds a number of new views and view features. Even Normal view—the home base in which most users develop presentation content and slide design—includes a couple of new tricks.

In new presentations, the Notes pane in which you add speaker notes might not initially appear. By leaving the Notes pane

closed, you can zoom the Slide pane to a larger size when you're working with slide design. But, when you need to add your notes, you can display the Notes pane and use it. After you display the Notes pane, it remains open any time you work in the presentation file, until you close the pane. Similarly, you might not need to see the slide thumbnails in the Thumbnails pane at the left side of the view. You can collapse it when you want to focus on how the current slide looks and re-expand it to navigate the presentation

Show or hide the Notes pane

1 On the ribbon, click the View tab.

2 In the Show group, click Notes.

   The Notes pane appears below the current slide in the Slides pane.

3 Drag the Notes pane divider up to enlarge the notes area.

4 Click in the Notes pane and then type your speaker notes for the current slide.

5 Click Notes again to hide the Notes pane.

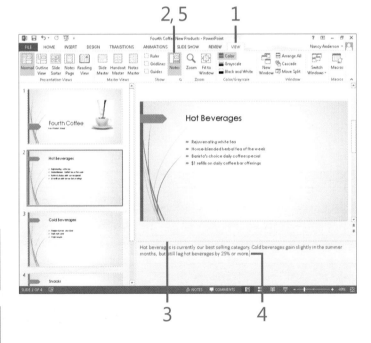

> **SEE ALSO** The Notes pane is also available in Outline view. To learn more about Outline view, see "Working with the outline" on page 99.

> **TIP** Click Notes on the status bar to hide and redisplay the Notes pane.

Control the Thumbnails pane

1 Move the mouse pointer over the divider at the right side of the Thumbnails pane and drag all the way to the left. The pane collapses into a bar labeled Thumbnails at the top.

2 Click the right-arrow button above Thumbnails in the bar.

The pane reopens, displaying slide thumbnails.

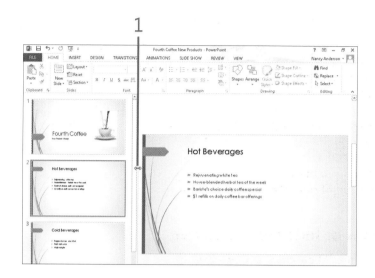

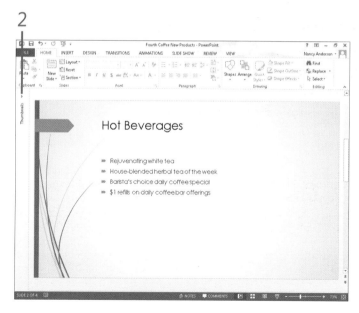

SEE ALSO Outline view also includes a pane at the left called—not surprisingly—the Outline pane. You can use the same steps here to close and redisplay that pane. To learn more about Outline view, see "Working with the outline" on page 99.

TIP Most views include the new resume reading feature. When you reopen the presentation, a pop-up window at the right on the vertical scroll bar asks if you want to go back to the slide you were on when you last saved the presentation. Click anywhere in the pop-up window to jump to the slide.

Using other new view features

PowerPoint 2013 includes two additional features that help you to work more effectively. You can now set the ribbon to behave in three different ways: you can auto-hide it so that you have to click at the top of PowerPoint to see the ribbon; you can also set the ribbon to display as tabs only; and you can set it in the default view with both tabs and commands. Also, the Normal and Reading views now include a helpful feature. When you reopen a presentation, a pop-up window appears near the vertical scroll bar that offers to bring you to the slide you were working on when you last saved and closed the presentation.

Control ribbon display

1 In the upper-right corner of the PowerPoint screen, beside the window controls, click the Ribbon Display Options button.

2 Click the display mode to use for the ribbon.

3 Repeat steps 1 and 2 as needed to change to a different ribbon behavior.

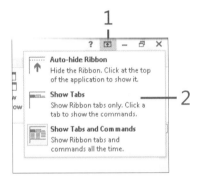

> **TRY THIS!** You can press Ctrl+F1 to collapse and redisplay the ribbon.

Start working at the previous slide

1 Open the presentation.

2 Click the Welcome Back! pop-up message that appears at the right side of the view.

   PowerPoint displays the slide you were working on when you last saved and then closed the presentation.

> **SEE ALSO** To learn more about the various views, see "Moving among views" on page 53.

Commenting and using widescreen

PowerPoint 2013 now gathers reviewer comments in a central Comments pane for faster collaboration. Use the Comments pane to add and delete comments as well as reply to comments from others who have reviewed the presentation.

With the growing adoption of the widescreen format for monitors, projectors, TVs, and other displays, PowerPoint 2013 now uses the wide 16:9 slide format by default for every new slide show. This means that you can take advantage of the expanded screen size as you develop your presentation and have a clear picture of what it will look like when played for your audience. When necessary, you can change slides back to the traditional 4:3 aspect ratio.

Use the new Comments pane

1 On the ribbon, click the Review tab.

2 In the Comments group, click Show Comments.

The Comments pane appears at the right side of your screen.

3 Click Next to display the next comment in the presentation, even if it's on another slide.

4 Click Previous to move to the previous comment, even if it's on another slide.

5 Click New and type your text to add a new comment.

(continued on next page)

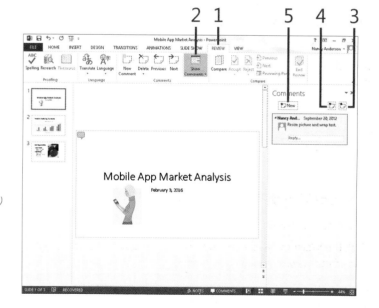

TIP When you're using the Next and Previous buttons to navigate comments, a message box informs you when there are no more comments to review. Click Cancel to finish navigating the comments.

Use the new Comments pane *(continued)*

6 Click Reply below an existing comment, type your reply text, and then press Enter.

7 Click Show Comments. Or you could click the Comments pane window close button. The Comments pane closes.

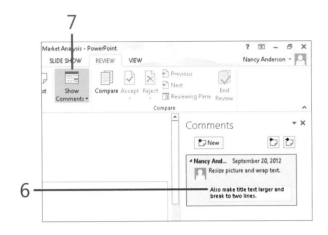

Work in 16:9 format

1 On the ribbon, click the Design tab.

2 In the Customize group, click Slide Size.

The available slide sizes appear.

3 Click the slide size to use for your presentation.

PowerPoint 2013 creates new presentations in the Widescreen (16:9) size by default, but you can change back to the Standard (4:3) size if that better suits your display, projection, or TV equipment.

4 In the dialog box that asks how to scale slide content based on the new slide size, click either Maximize or Ensure Fit.

The Ensure Fit choice enlarges slide content to fill the slide size and some content may be cut off; Minimize reduces the size of slide content to fit on the new slide size.

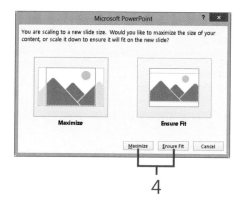

> **TIP** Standard format slides will play on a widescreen display, and vice versa. However, when you play a presentation formatted for widescreen on a monitor, projector, or TV with a standard screen, black bars will fill the area above and below the slide on screen.

Incorporating online pictures

PowerPoint 2013 connects you directly with online resources for finding digital content to add to your presentations. You can search for royalty-free pictures through the Office.com Clip Art collection or Bing search. You can also download pictures from your SkyDrive or an online photo service such as Flickr. You can take advantage of this expanded new resource to make your slides come alive visually.

Insert online pictures

1 On the ribbon, click the Insert tab.

2 In the Images group, click Online Pictures.

3 In the Insert Pictures window, type a search term in the Office.com Clip Art search box.

4 Click the Search button or press Enter.

The Office.com Clip Art window shows pictures and illustrations matching the search term. Scroll down the list to see the results.

(continued on next page)

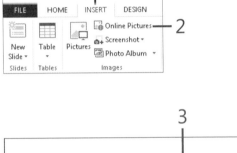

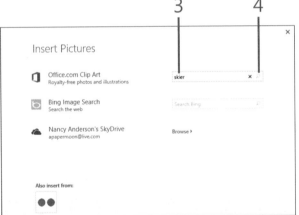

> ➔ **TRY THIS!** The Picture Tools|Format contextual tab appears any time you select an inserted picture. Try inserting a clip-art image by using the Online Pictures button on the Insert tab. Leave the image selected and then explore the tools available on the Picture Tools|Format contextual tab. You can learn more about these in Section 11, "Formatting text and objects," starting on page 165.

Insert online pictures *(continued)*

5 Click the picture to insert.

6 Click Insert.

7 Drag the picture into position on the slide.

8 Click the slide background to deselect the picture.

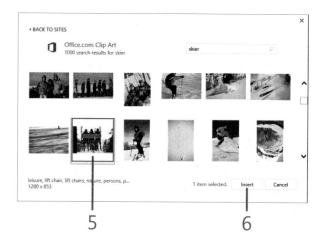

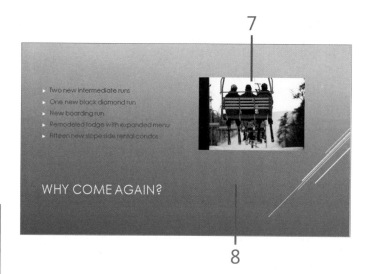

Including online video and audio

Similar to finding online clip art, you can search for digital video and audio to include for playback during a PowerPoint 2013 slide show. The Office.com Clip Art collection also includes royalty-free audio, and you can search for video on Bing or insert it from YouTube and other video sites. Later sections provide more details, but here you get a look at each of these new features.

Insert online video

1   On the ribbon, click the Insert tab.

2   In the Media group, click Video, and then in the drop-down list that appears, click Online Video.

3   In the Insert Video window, type a search term in the Bing Video Search box.

4   Click the Search button or press Enter.

The Bing Video Search window shows videos matching the search term. Scroll down the list to see the results.

(continued on next page)

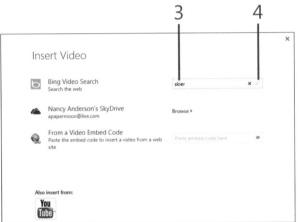

> **TRY THIS!**   Insert a video by using the Online Video choice after clicking Video on the Insert tab. To play the video, double-click it to display the playback controls. Click the Play button that appears in the middle of the video to start playing the video.

> **TIP**   When a video is selected on a slide, the Video Tools|Format and Video Tools|Playback contextual tabs appear. On the Video Tools|Format tab, you can apply different corrections and effects to the video, such as correcting the color, recoloring the video, adding a frame, or adding a style. The Video Tools|Playback tab lets you trim the video, fade it in and out, and more.

Insert online video *(continued)*

5 Click the video that you want to insert.

6 Click Insert. From there, you can drag the video into position on the slide.

5

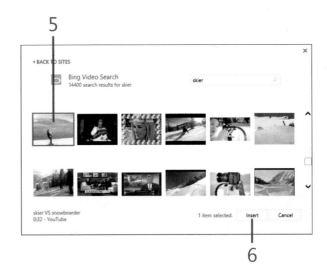

6

Insert online audio

1 On the ribbon, click the Insert tab.

2 In the Media group, click Audio, and then in the drop-down list that appears, click Online Audio.

(continued on next page)

1   2

> **TIP** The audio clip appears as an icon on the slide. To hide the icon display, on the Audio Tools|Playback contextual tab, in the Audio Options group, select the Hide During Show check box. If you do this, in the same group you might also want to select Start and then Automatically to ensure that the sound plays during the show.

Insert online audio _(continued)_

3 In the Insert Audio window, type a search term in the Office.com Clip Art search box.

4 Click the Search button or press Enter.

The Office.com Clip Art window shows audio clips matching the search term. Scroll down the list to see the results.

5 Click the audio clip that you want to insert.

6 Click Insert. From there, you can drag the clip icon into position on the slide.

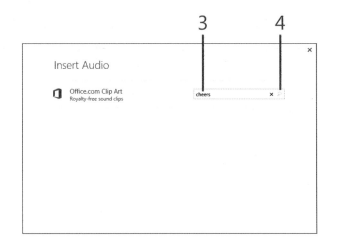

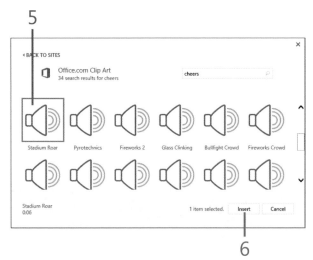

> **TRY THIS!** Insert an audio clip by using the Online Audio choice after clicking Audio on the Insert tab. To play the audio, move the mouse pointer over it to display the playback controls. Click the Play button that appears at the left end of the bar to play the audio.

Taking advantage of theme variants, Smart Guides, and merge shapes

PowerPoint 2013 brings you fresh, modernized themes that make any presentation look and feel more current. Each theme now includes a group of theme variants or variations; you can choose a variant to apply a new color scheme to the presentation. As you design your slides, Smart Guides (sometimes also called alignment guides) appear to help you align objects and text for a more polished result. You also can merge a group of selected shapes to create your own custom shape that's easier to move and format.

Preview and select a theme variant

1 On the ribbon, click the Design tab.

2 In the Variants group, move your mouse pointer over the variants.

Each in turn is previewed on your slide presentation.

3 Click a variant to apply it your entire presentation.

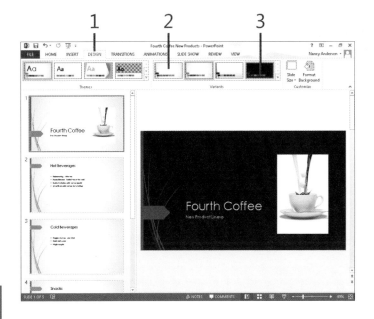

> **SEE ALSO** For more information about working with themes and other design elements, see Section 9, "Adjusting slide appearance," starting on page 117.

> **TIP** Themes were introduced in PowerPoint 2007, and Microsoft offers the option of expanding your theme horizons by searching for new themes after you click the File tab and then click New.

Use Smart Guides

1 To move an object, click the object to select it.

2 Drag the object toward the text or other object to which you want to align it.

When the object is in alignment, the Smart Guides appear. Dashed-red horizontal and dashed-gray vertical lines show you when the object is aligned horizontally or vertically with respect to other objects and text, and when it is centered relative to text. Dashed-red arrows indicate the relative widths of text and objects to help you balance the slide composition.

3 When the guides show that the object is in the desired position, release the mouse button.

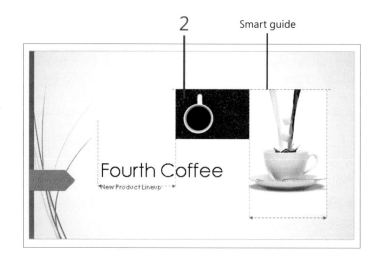

2

Smart guide

Fourth Coffee

New Product Lineup

TRY THIS! As you drag an object around, Smart Guides might appear at unexpected locations. Smart Guides suggest positions that work in terms of good graphic design. Try dropping an object into an alternative spot suggested by the guides to see the design effect.

Merge shapes

1 Create and format a number of shapes and arrange them to make a more complex graphic.

2 Shift+click each of the shapes or drag over them to select them all.

3 On the ribbon, click the Drawing Tools|Format contextual tab if it is not selected.

4 In the Insert Shapes group, click the Merge Shapes button and move your mouse pointer over the various merge choices to see them previewed on the selected shapes.

5 Click a merge choice to apply it.

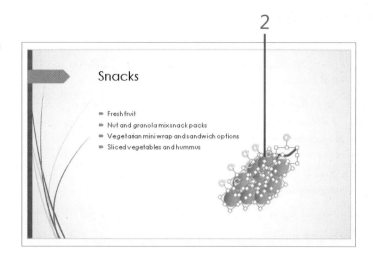

TIP You can change the fill and formatting for the merged object.

SEE ALSO To get the effect you want in the merged object, you might need to experiment quite a bit with the shape fills and how you layer the individual shapes. You can learn how to work with these shape settings and more in Section 11, "Formatting Text and Objects," on page 165.

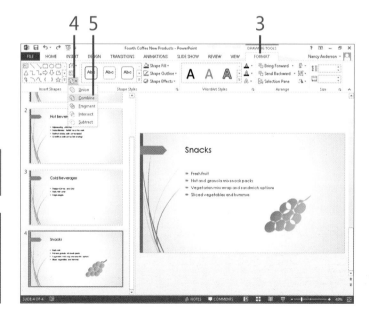

Working in the cloud

PowerPoint 2013 works seamlessly with the online SkyDrive storage you receive free with the Microsoft Account you use to sign in to Windows and Office 2013. When you store a presentation in your SkyDrive folders in the cloud, it automatically syncs to your local SkyDrive folders (assuming you have the SkyDrive for Windows installed, if needed) so that you can easily open the presentation on other devices and share it with other users.

Save a presentation to your SkyDrive

1 On the ribbon, click the File tab to display the Backstage view.

2 Click Save As.

3 On the Save As screen, in the middle section, click your SkyDrive.

4 Click Browse.

The Save As dialog box opens.

5 Choose another folder on your SkyDrive to which to save, if needed. To do this, under Favorites, click SkyDrive and then double-click one of the folders that appears.

6 Edit the file name if needed.

7 Click Save.

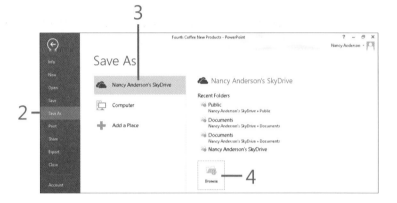

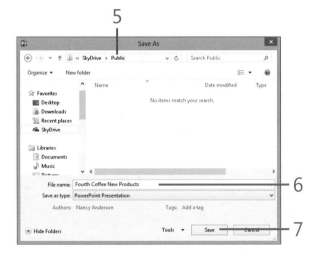

TIP If your Microsoft and Office accounts are set up correctly, SkyDrive automatically synchronizes files between the SkyDrive folders on your computer or device and those on your account in the cloud. To check on the setup in PowerPoint, click the File tab and then click Account. Ensure that your SkyDrive account appears under Connected Services. You can open files from your SkyDrive, too. Just click Open instead of Save As in step 2.

Share a presentation from your SkyDrive

1 Save the File to share to your SkyDrive, as described in the previous task, and then leave the file open in PowerPoint.

2 On the ribbon, click the File tab to display the Backstage view.

3 Click Share.

4 In the Share section, click Invite People.

5 In the Type Names Or E-Mail Addresses text box, enter contact email addresses.

6 Type a message about the shared file, if you want.

7 Click Share.

After SkyDrive sends the invitation, the name of each user with whom you've shared the document appears under Shared With at the bottom of the Share screen.

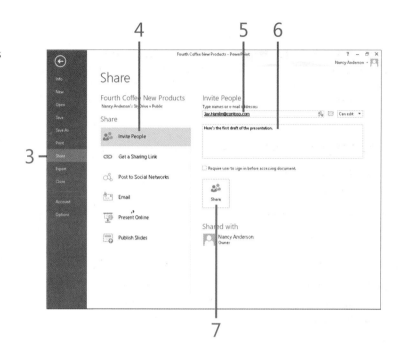

TIP Select the Require User To Sign-In Before Accessing Documents check box when sharing highly sensitive documents which you want only authorized users to see.

Presenting slide shows

PowerPoint 2013 introduces an enhanced version of Presenter view. This is a view that you use to control the slide show on one monitor while simultaneously displaying the show on another monitor or projector. When you broadcast a presentation, you make it available as a live presentation that others can view by using their web browsers. The process is even more simple in PowerPoint 2013, which doesn't require you to have your own site to host the presentation. It's an excellent way to give a live presentation to remote viewers. Get started with both of these updated features now.

Using the improved Presenter view

1 On the ribbon, click the Slide Show tab.

Be sure that you've connected and set up the second monitor or projector before starting this process.

2 In the Monitors group, select the Use Presenter View check box.

3 In the Start Slide Show group, click From Beginning.

4 To run the show, use the controls that appear, and look at the Notes pane at lower right to see any speaker notes that you've entered for the currently displayed slide.

5 Click End Slide Show to finish the show.

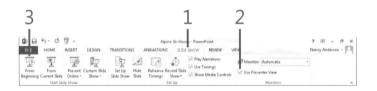

> **TRY THIS!** If you don't see Presenter view because you don't have two monitors attached to your system, press Alt+F5 to start the slide show and display Presenter view.

Presenting online

1 On the ribbon, click the File tab to display the Backstage view.

2 Click Share.

3 Click Present Online under Share.

4 Click the Present Online button that appears. Enter your Microsoft Account user ID and password, if requested, and click Sign In. PowerPoint connects to the Office Presentation Service and prepares the presentation for online broadcast.

5 In the Present Online window that appears, click Copy Link to copy the web address and paste it into an email invitation yourself, or click Send In Email to simply open an email message and send the link.

6 Click the Start Presentation button to use the default Office Presentation Service to broadcast the presentation to the invited users.

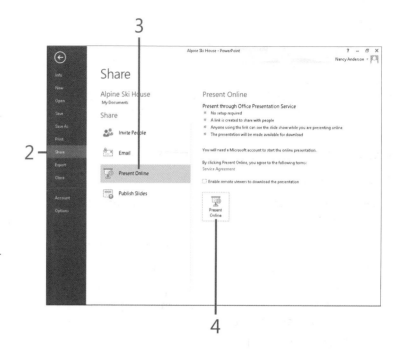

 **SEE ALSO** For more information on this feature, see Section 16, "Sharing a Presentation," starting on page 251.

Getting started with PowerPoint 2013

3

Microsoft PowerPoint 2013 sports the same user interface that was introduced in PowerPoint 2007—with some slight changes. After investing a little time getting used to the new tools and features, you'll find that this version of PowerPoint is actually easier to use. This section helps you to explore and learn to use the most essential tools in PowerPoint 2013.

Clicking the PowerPoint File tab displays what is known as the Backstage view. It's here where you'll find file-management commands such as New, Open, Save, and Print. Other than the File tab, most features are available on the ribbon, gathered on tabs that present related command buttons. Which tools are available depends on what tab you've selected, which, in turn, depends on what you're trying to do. In some cases, you will work with contextual tools such as the mini toolbar and panes that appear when you select particular commands for research or formatting.

You will work with galleries of graphical selections, which you use to preview effects such as animations before you apply them. Themes and variants give you the power to change the look of the entire presentation with just a few mouse clicks. Finally, PowerPoint provides tools that supply help when needed and provide instructions for performing a variety of tasks.

In this section:

- What's where in PowerPoint 2013?
- Using the ribbon
- Working with the mini toolbar
- Customizing the Quick Access Toolbar
- Applying design choices
- Updating a presentation with a theme and a variant
- Getting help

What's where in PowerPoint 2013?

PowerPoint 2013 provides a central ribbon of tools on which you can select various tabs. The tools on the tabs are organized into groups. In addition, the Quick Access Toolbar lets you place your favorite tools in one location and access functions that aren't offered on the ribbon. Some tools on the ribbon offer drop-down galleries of selections or menus with additional choices; other tools open dialog boxes in which you can configure detailed settings. When you select an object on a slide, the ribbon presents a *contextual tab* that offers even more tools for working with that object.

You access the file choices by clicking the File tab located at the far left on the ribbon. This displays the Backstage view, where you can choose several common file commands from among the tabs presented on the left side of the screen or click the Options tab to open a dialog box which contains a wealth of setting options that you can use to control the way PowerPoint works and how you interact with it. To exit the Backstage view and redisplay the ribbon and presentation, at the top of the fle tab choices click the left-arrow button.

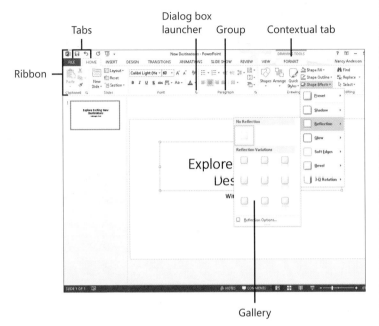

TIP Just as with Windows 8, PowerPoint 2013 works best when you sign in with a Microsoft account. The name of the signed-in user appears in the upper-right corner of PowerPoint. You can click the down-arrow beside the user name to access commands for changing account settings, switching accounts, and more.

Using the ribbon

The ribbon is your control center in PowerPoint 2013. The default ribbon consists of nine tabs, although contextual tabs appear now and then when you work with certain types of objects or functions. An additional tab, Add-Ins, appears if you install PowerPoint Extras or third-party programs that enhance PowerPoint.

Display tabs and panes

1 On the ribbon, click the Review tab.

2 In the Proofing group, click Research to open the Research pane.

3 Click the Close button (the "x" in the upper-right of the pane) to close the pane.

(continued on next page)

> **TRY THIS!** You can open dialog boxes associated with groups of tools by clicking the dialog box launcher, which is the small arrow located in the lower-right corner of many groups on the ribbon. This displays additional settings and features related to the ribbon functions.

> **TIP** To find out what a tool on the ribbon does, move the mouse pointer over it. A ScreenTip appears, showing the name of the tool and a keyboard shortcut (when one exists). For example, if you place your pointer over the Paste button, you'll see Ctrl+V in parentheses after the tool name in the ScreenTip. You can use this keyboard combination to paste an item instead of clicking the button. If you click File and then click Options, you can use the ScreenTip style drop-down list on the General tab of the PowerPoint Options dialog box to control the level of detail in the ScreenTips. Click OK to apply your choice.

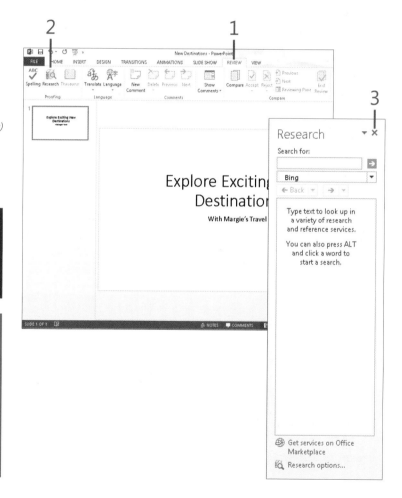

Display tabs and panes *(continued)*

4 Click the Insert tab.

5 In the Illustrations group, click the Shapes button and then click an item in the Shapes group.

6 Drag anywhere on the slide to draw the shape.

7 Note that the Drawing Tools|Format contextual tab appears. This is due to the type of object that's selected. Click the tab to reveal options for formatting the selected shape.

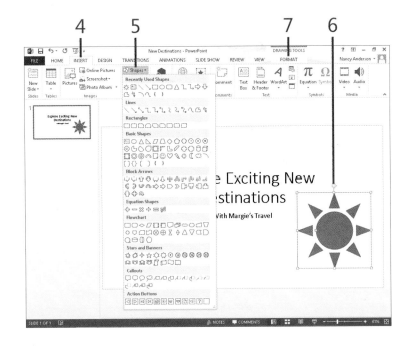

TIP To include add-in programs, click the File tab, click Options, and then in the PowerPoint Options dialog box, click the Add-Ins tab. For example, you can include additional presenter tools or presentation notes tools.

TIP Can't find a tool? Some tools, such as AutoCorrect Options, are not on the ribbon. In this case, you have to add the tools to the Quick Access Toolbar to perform the function. See "Customizing the Quick Access Toolbar" on page 40 for more about how to do this.

Working with the mini toolbar

Everybody who has ever worked on any kind of document, from a word-processed letter to a PowerPoint presentation, knows that formatting text is one of the most frequent tasks you perform. That is perhaps why Microsoft created the mini toolbar.

When you select text, a small, floating toolbar appears next to the text itself. You can easily click tools such as Bold, Italic, or Font Size without having to move your mouse pointer up to the ribbon and back to the text again.

Display and use the mini toolbar

1 Select text on a slide.

The mini toolbar appears next to the text.

2 Move the mouse pointer over the mini toolbar and click a tool.

3 Move the mouse pointer away from the mini toolbar.

The mini toolbar disappears.

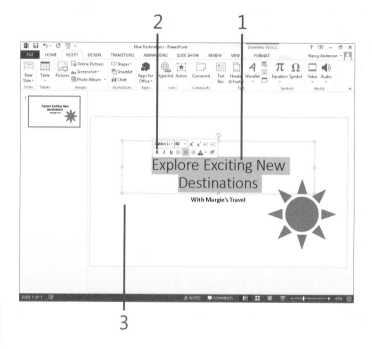

> **SEE ALSO** For more information about working with text formatting tools that appear both on the Home tab of the ribbon and on the mini toolbar, see Section 11, "Formatting text and objects," starting on page 165.

> **TIP** If you accidentally move the mouse pointer away from the mini toolbar, you must select the text again to make the toolbar reappear.

Customizing the Quick Access Toolbar

The idea behind the interface that Microsoft Office 2007 introduced is that the most commonly used tools are present on the ribbon rather than buried in dialog boxes, and the tools you use less often, though accessible, aren't part of the main interface by default. Sometimes the only way to access a function you might have used in previous versions of PowerPoint is to place a command on the Quick Access Toolbar. By default this toolbar contains only the Save, Undo, Redo, and Start From Beginning commands, but you can add as many commands as you want.

Add and arrange Quick Access toolbar buttons

1 On the ribbon, click the File tab to display the Backstage view and then choose Options.

The PowerPoint Options dialog box opens.

2 In the menu at the left of the window, click Quick Access Toolbar.

3 In the Choose Commands From list, click the down-arrow and select a category of tools, or click the list, press the Down Arrow key once, and press Enter to choose the Commands Not In The Ribbon category.

(continued on next page)

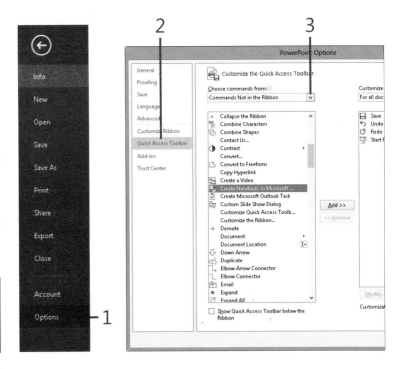

> ✓ **TIP** You can remove a button from the Quick Access toolbar without using the PowerPoint Options dialog box. To do so, right-click the button on the toolbar, and then in the shortcut menu that appears, click Remove From Quick Access Toolbar.

> ⚠ **CAUTION** Although you can add many tools to the toolbar, don't overdo it. Only add the tools that you use most often, or add a tool to use a particular function and then remove it to clear clutter off the toolbar.

Add and arrange Quick Access Toolbar
buttons *(continued)*

4 Click a command in the list on the left and then click the Add button to add it to the toolbar. Repeat this step for all the commands that you want to add.

5 Click a command in the list on the right and then click one of the arrow buttons to the right to move the command up or down. Moving a tool up moves it further left on the Quick Access Toolbar.

6 Click OK.

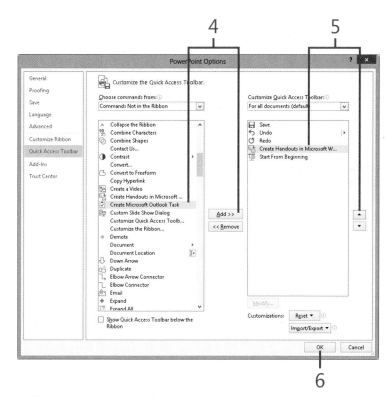

The tool added to the toolbar.

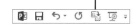

> ✓ **TIP** If you fill up your Quick Access Toolbar and want to put it back the way it was when you first installed PowerPoint, go to the PowerPoint Options dialog box and click Quick Access Toolbar. Click Reset and then click Reset Only Quick Access Toolbar. After you click OK, the default tools reappear on the toolbar.

> ✓ **TIP** If you want to add some space between sets of tools on the Quick Access Toolbar, at the top of the list on the left of the Quick Access Toolbar window, simply click the item labeled <Separator> and then click Add.

Applying design choices

The Live Preview feature in PowerPoint 2013 makes it easy to design your presentation text and graphics. Galleries of predesigned formats help you to browse through different styles and preview how each looks in your presentation.

Preview and apply design elements with galleries

1 Click a placeholder on a slide, enter some text, and then select the text.

2 On the ribbon, click the Drawing Tools|Format contextual tab.

3 Click the More arrow at the lower right of the WordArt Styles gallery.

4 Move your mouse pointer over the various WordArt styles.

5 You can see each style previewed on the selected text. Click a style to apply it.

(continued on next page)

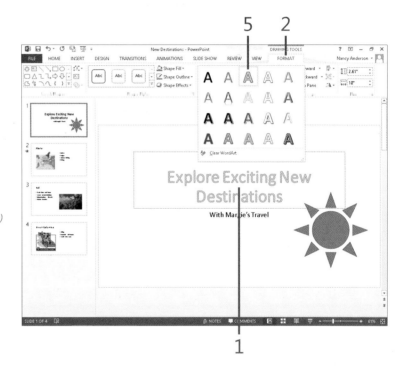

✓ TIP   Several galleries exist on tabs that don't appear until you insert certain types of objects such as pictures or drawings. Although the Drawing Tools|Format tab contains an Insert Shapes group, there is also a Shapes gallery on the Insert tab, which you can use to draw shapes on your slides when the Format tab isn't available.

Preview and apply design elements with galleries *(continued)*

6 Click the Home tab and then click the down-arrow on the Font list.

7 Move your mouse pointer down the list of fonts.

You can see each font previewed on the selected text. Click a font to apply it.

TRY THIS! You can preview font sizes on selected text. With text selected, click the down-arrow on the Font Size list and move your mouse pointer down the list of sizes. Each is previewed on your text.

SEE ALSO For more information about WordArt and other drawing objects, see Section 10, "Inserting media and drawing objects," starting on page 127.

Updating a presentation with a theme and a variant

PowerPoint 2013 brings you fresh, modernized themes that make any presentation feel more current. Each theme now includes a group of theme variants, which you can choose to apply a new color scheme to the presentation. Change the theme or pick a variant to give a fresh new look to every slide in your presentation.

Apply a theme and variant

1 On the ribbon, click the Design tab.

2 Click the down-arrow to the right of the Themes gallery.

3 Scroll if needed, and move your mouse pointer over the various themes. You can see each one previewed on your slide presentation.

4 Click a theme to apply it to your entire presentation.

5 Move your mouse pointer over the available variants in the Variants gallery. You can see each one previewed on your slide presentation.

6 Click a variant to apply it to your entire presentation.

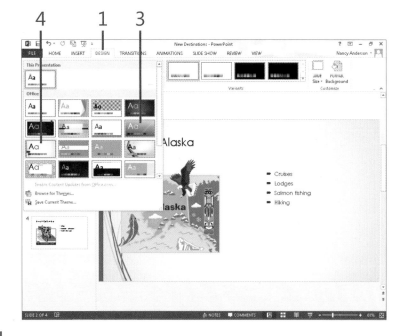

SEE ALSO   For more information about working with themes and other design elements, see Section 9, "Adjusting slide appearance," starting on page 117.

TIP   If more variants are available, the Variants gallery scroll buttons become active so that you can scroll to see additional choices.

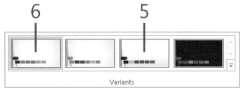

Getting Help

PowerPoint 2013 includes both offline Help, in the form of a searchable database of information, and online Help, which provides even more information from Office.com. By learning how to use PowerPoint Help, you can solve small problems that you might run into and delve deeper into PowerPoint features.

Use Help

1 Click the Microsoft PowerPoint Help button to display the Power-Point Help window.

2 Enter a search term and click Search.

3 Click a topic in the list of search results to view the Help information.

4 Click the Home button to go to the main listing of topics at any time.

5 Click the Print button to print the currently displayed topic.

> ⚠ **CAUTION** If you want to keep the Help window visible as you work in your presentation, click the Pin Help button before clicking within the document.

Creating presentations

4

Whether you want to create a lengthy, elaborate, animated presentation with sound and graphics or a simple presentation consisting of a bulleted list and a handful of slides, your first steps are to learn how to open a blank presentation and to understand the basic structure of a standard Microsoft PowerPoint 2013 presentation.

You can open a blank presentation, open presentations you have previously created and saved, or create presentations based on templates that provide prebuilt design features. After you open a file, you can enter content for a presentation. Later, if you make changes, you need to know how to save those changes and close the presentation.

As you wander around PowerPoint, you will become acquainted with the different views you use to accomplish various tasks. When you open a presentation, it opens in Normal view, wherein you see two panes, one showing thumbnails of all the slides in the presentation, and the other pane, in which the current slide is displayed. You optionally can display a pane for notes.

You can display a presentation in Full Screen mode. Or, you can use the new Reading view to proofread it at your own pace. Slide Sorter view is convenient for organizing slides. And, when you want to see your slide show in action, use Slide Show view.

In this section:

- Creating a presentation
- Finding and opening existing presentations
- Moving among views
- Using Reading view
- Sizing panes in Normal view
- Viewing multiple slides in Slide Sorter view
- Running a presentation in Slide Show view
- Saving a PowerPoint presentation
- Closing a PowerPoint presentation

Creating a presentation

PowerPoint 2013 offers a few options to get you started with a new presentation. For example, if you want a single, blank slide with the default layout and design elements, you can open a blank presentation or one that is based on a PowerPoint theme. If you want to get a head start on your presentation, consider basing it on one of the online templates that you can download.

Open a blank presentation or one with a theme

1 With PowerPoint running, click the File tab to display the Backstage view and then select the New tab to open the New window.

2 Click Blank Presentation or one of the available themes.

If you select a theme, a window of variant choices appears.

3 Click a variant.

4 Click Create.

TIP If you prefer to open a file by using a keyboard shortcut, you can press Ctrl+O to display the Open dialog box or Ctrl+N to open a new blank presentation.

Open a template

1 With PowerPoint running and your computer connected to the Internet, click the File tab to display the Backstage view and then select the New tab to open the New window.

2 Click one of the suggested searches or type your own search term in the Search Online Templates And Themes text box and press Enter.

3 Click a category in the Category list at the right to filter the results further, if desired, and scroll to display the matching templates.

4 Click a template.

   A description of the template appears.

5 Click Create to download the template and open a new file based on it.

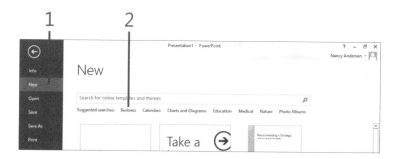

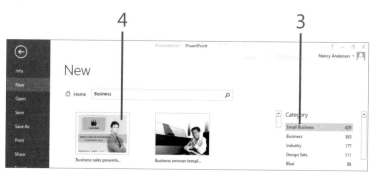

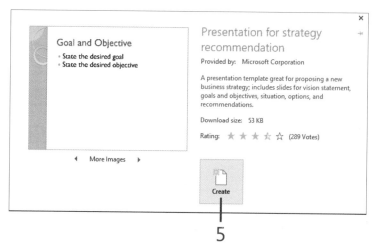

SEE ALSO Any theme used by the template you apply to your presentation is accessible in the Themes gallery on the Design tab. For information about applying themes to slides, see "Working with themes" on page 120.

Finding and opening existing presentations

Very often, putting together a presentation involves several work sessions. Perhaps you enter slide text in one sitting, tweak the arrangement of graphics and colors in another, and still later edit what you created to incorporate others' feedback or to

proof for spelling errors. Every time you want to make a change, you need to open the existing presentation. You can open files stored on your computer's hard disk, removable storage media such as USB stick, a shared network location, or your SkyDrive.

Open a presentation

1 On the ribbon, click the File tab to display the Backstage view and then select the Open tab.

2 Under Open, click Computer.

3 In the Current Folder or Recent Folders section, click one of the folders or click Browse.

(continued on next page)

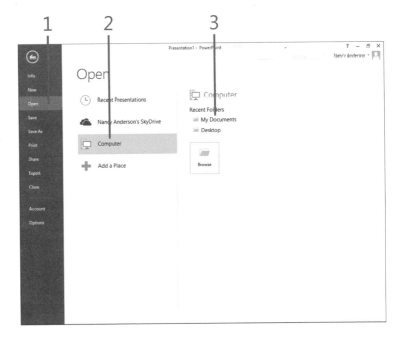

TIP You can use the buttons along the left side of the Open dialog box to find a file more quickly. For example, if you just downloaded the file recently, open the Downloads location; if the file is stored in a shared folder on a network, open the Network choice; and so on.

Open a presentation *(continued)*

4 In the navigation pane on the left, double-click a location to browse available local, online, and network drives and folders. Continue to double-click folders until you find the one that contains the file you want.

5 Click a folder to open it and display its files in the file list.

6 You might need to specify the file type for the document that you want to locate; All PowerPoint Presentations is the default format. Only documents saved in the specified file format are displayed in the file list.

7 Click a file and then click Open.

The Open dialog box appears.

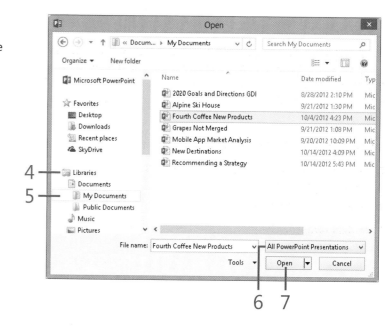

TIP If you used a file recently, in the Backstage view, choose the Open command on the File tab, click Recent Presentations under Places, and then just click the desired file to open it.

Open a presentation from your SkyDrive

1 On the ribbon, click the File tab to display the Backstage view and then select the Open tab.

2 Under Open click your SkyDrive.

3 In the Recent Folders section, click one of the folders or click Browse.

4 If needed, use the navigation pane and the file list to browse other folders within your SkyDrive folder.

5 Click a file and then click Open.

The Open dialog box appears.

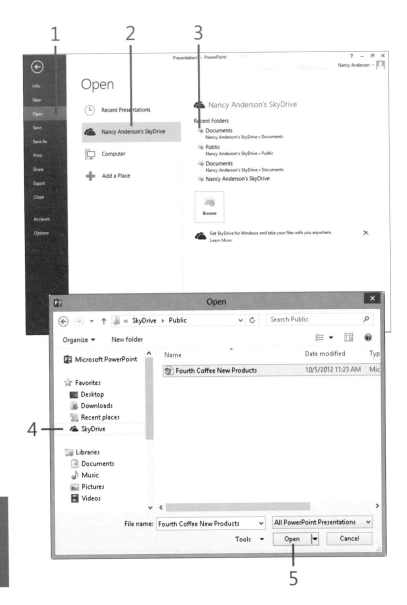

TIP The SkyDrive folder you select when you open and save files is actually a folder on your computer. PowerPoint uses your Microsoft account information to automatically synchronize files in the local SkyDrive folder to your online SkyDrive folder. That way you can use any Internet-connected device to access the file.

Moving among views

PowerPoint 2013 offers several views with which you can focus on different aspects of your presentation. You can access four of the views—Normal, Slide Sorter, Reading, and Slide Show—from buttons on the status bar located along the bottom of the PowerPoint window; you can access another view, Notes Page, on the View tab. Note that these buttons do not appear when your presentation is in Slide Show, Reading view, or Full Screen mode. You must exit the slide show or the mode to use them. You will learn more about how each view is used throughout this section.

Slide Show view

Normal view

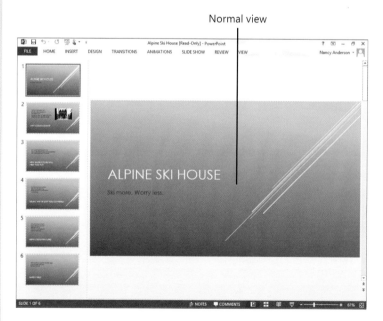

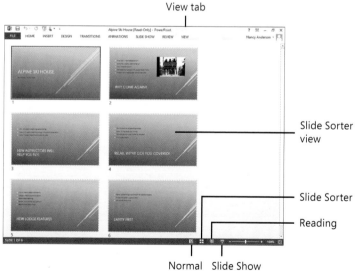

View tab

Slide Sorter view

Slide Sorter

Reading

Normal   Slide Show

Using Reading view

Reading view works like an onscreen slide show, displaying one slide at a time in large size while giving you control to move slide by slide at your own reading speed. This can be very helpful as you proofread your work, but be aware that you cannot edit slides in Reading view. The status bar remains on the screen, however, so if you do see a typo, you can click the Normal button there, edit the slide in Normal view, and then return to Reading view.

Use Reading view

1 On the ribbon, click the View tab.

2 In the Presentation Views group, click Reading View.

The first slide of your presentation appears onscreen.

3 To advance through the slides, press Spacebar or click the slide. You also can use the Preview or Next buttons on the status bar to move among slides.

4 At the End Of Slide Show message, press Esc or click to return to the prior view.

> ✓ **TIP** If you prefer to use Reading view with the title bar and status bar hidden, you can do that, as well. Click the Menu button on the status bar or right-click anywhere on the current slide. On the shortcut menu that appears, click Full Screen. Click or press Spacebar to advance from slide to slide. To reveal controls for working with the slide show, move the mouse pointer over the lower-left corner of the slide. Press Esc to redisplay the title bar and status bar in Reading view.

> ✓ **TIP** While in Reading view, you can right-click a slide to display a shortcut menu that contains commands for controlling the show, including exiting. You can press Esc any time to exit, too.

2   1

3

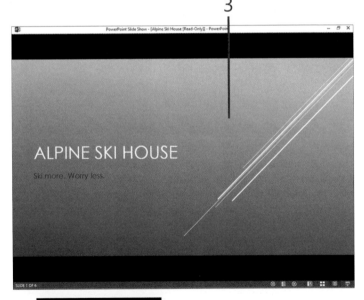

ALPINE SKI HOUSE

Ski more. Worry less.

4 —

End of slide show, click to exit.

Sizing panes in Normal view

Typically, you will do most of your work building your presentation in Normal view. This view consists of three panes: the Thumbnails pane gives you access to tabs that provide an overview of your presentation; the Notes pane is where you enter speaker notes to help guide you as you give your presentation; and the Slides pane is where you work on the design of an individual slide. The Notes pane might not display when you initially create a presentation, but you can display it when needed. You can temporarily remove the Thumbnails and Notes panes, or you can resize them to focus on one aspect of your presentation.

Resize a pane

1 Move your mouse pointer over the edge of the Thumbnails or Notes pane (the boundary between it and the adjacent pane).

2 When the pointer turns into a horizontal double-headed arrow, drag the pane divider in the desired direction to make the pane larger or smaller.

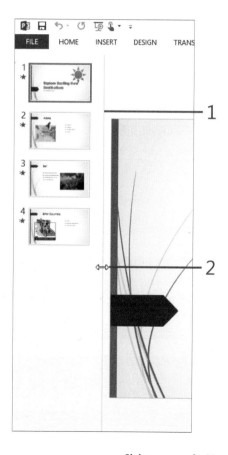

> ✓ **TIP** If you drag a pane divider until the pane disappears, the divider is still visible. You can drag the divider to display the pane again. Note that the Thumbnails pane on the left side of Normal view can be resized to a maximum width of about 4 inches.

> ✓ **TIP** You can change how large the slide preview appears in the Slides pane without resizing the pane by dragging the zoom slider at the bottom of the PowerPoint window. To refit the slide to the Slides pane in Normal view after you change its zoom setting, click the Fit Slide To Current Window button, which is located to the right of the Zoom slider. The Fit Slide To Current Window button does not appear in any other view.

Close and redisplay the Thumbnails and Notes panes

1 Drag the divider for the Thumbnails pane all the way left to close the pane.

2 To redisplay the Thumbnails pane, at the top of the pane, click the right-arrow button.

3 On the View tab, in the Show group, click Notes to toggle the Notes pane opened and closed.

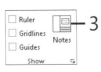

Clicking Normal on the View tab also reopens both the Thumbnails and Notes panes.

 SEE ALSO For information about working with the Slides tab, see Section 6, "Building a presentation," on page 81.

For information about working with the Outline feature, see Section 7, "Building a presentation outline," on page 97.

 TRY THIS! Take advantage of the ability to hide and resize panes to make your work easier. If you need to focus on slide design rather than on entering slide text, close the Thumbnails pane or make it smaller.

Viewing multiple slides in Slide Sorter view

After you create several slides, you might want to take your focus off an individual slide and look at your presentation as a whole. The best way to do this is to use Slide Sorter view, which displays all of your slides as thumbnails, placed in sequence from left to right. If you have many slides, they are arranged in rows. In this view, it's easy to locate a slide, rearrange slides to organize your slide show, or duplicate or delete slides.

Display Slide Sorter view and show more slides

1 On the View tab, click the Slide Sorter button.

2 Drag the Zoom slider on the status bar to the left to make the thumbnails smaller and fit more slides on the screen. Drag to the right to make the thumbnails larger, but with fewer of them on the screen.

Slide numbers are displayed beneath each slide.

This icon indicates that an animation or transition is applied to a slide.

Slide timings appear beneath slides if you have rehearsed the presentation and saved timings.

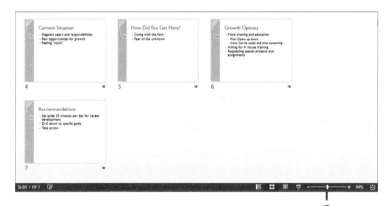

SEE ALSO You can do more than view slides in Slide Sorter view. You can delete, duplicate, hide, and reorder slides, as well as preview animations and more. See Section 8, "Managing and viewing slides," on page 107 for more features of this handy view.

Running a presentation in Slide Show view

Slide Show view is the one you use to run your presentation without the ribbon and status bar so that each slide fills the screen and viewers can focus on the presentation content. If you have your computer connected to a projector, television, or computer monitor, your audience can view your presentation by using a larger screen format than is available on your computer.

Slide Show view has several useful tools for navigating through your show, including a pen feature with which you can annotate your slides as you show them. You can even save your annotations at the end of the show.

Start, advance, and end

1. On the status bar, click the Slide Show view button to display the presentation, starting with the currently selected slide. You also can use the From Beginning button on the Slide Show tab to run the show.

2. On the keyboard, press the Left Arrow key to move back one slide, or press the Right Arrow key to move forward one slide.

(continued on next page)

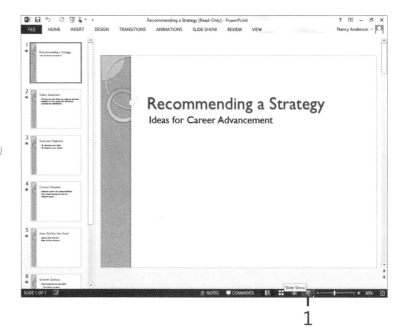

Start, advance, and end *(continued)*

3 With a presentation in Slide Show view, press Esc on your keyboard to end the slide show and return to the view displayed when you started the presentation (Normal or Slide Sorter).

4 If you created any annotations while running the show, a message box opens, asking whether you want to save your annotations. Click Keep or Discard, as desired.

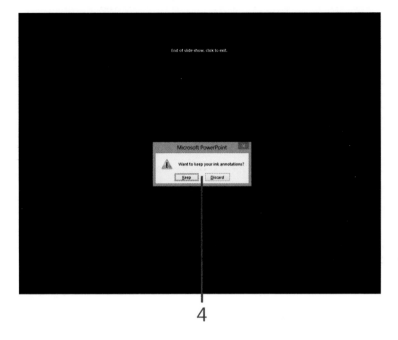

4

> ✓ **TIP** You can end a slide show at any point, whether you've reached the last slide or not, by using the method described here. If, however, you finish running through the slides in your show and reach the end, you see a message that the show is over. If you see that message, press any key to close the slide show.

> 🔍 **SEE ALSO** For information about using different methods to navigate through a slide show, including your mouse, onscreen buttons, and the Slide Show menu, see Section 14, "Running a presentation," on page 225. For information about setting up the way a slide show runs, see Section 13, "Finalizing your slide show," on page 207.

Saving a PowerPoint presentation

As you work on a presentation, you should save it periodically to avoid losing any of your work in the event of a computer crash or other problem. And, of course, you should also save any changes you want to keep before closing a file.

Save a presentation

1 On the ribbon, click the File tab to display the Backstage view and then select the Save As tab. You also can click Save.

For a new file, Save will display the Save As choices. For a previously saved file, Save adds your latest changes into the file, and you don't have to perform any further steps.

2 Under Save As, click Computer.

3 Click one of the folders under Recent Folders, or click Browse.

The Save As dialog box opens.

(continued on next page)

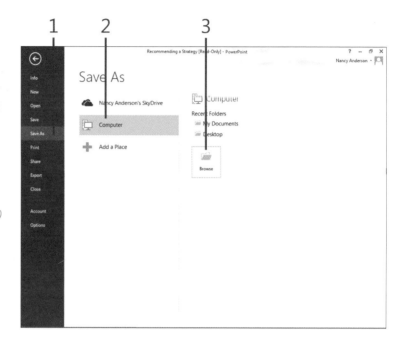

> **TRY THIS!** If you want to save a previously saved presentation with a new name, perhaps to use as the basis for another presentation, choose Save As from the File tab. Type a new file name and, if you want, locate another folder in which to save the file. Click Save to save a copy of the presentation with a new name.

Save a presentation *(continued)*

4 If you don't want to save the presentation to the default folder, select another drive or folder.

5 Type a name for the document of up to 255 characters; you cannot use the characters * : < > | " \ or /.

6 To save the document in a format other than the default Power-Point file format (.pptx), select a different format.

7 Click Save.

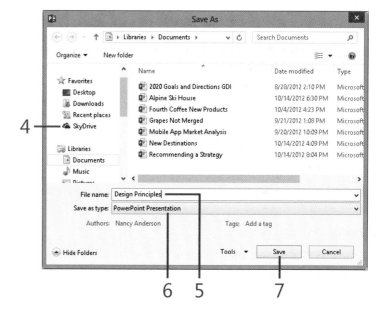

TIP To quickly save any changes to a previously saved document, simply click the Save button on the Quick Access Toolbar or press Ctrl+S. The file is saved without displaying the Save As dialog box.

TIP You can now save a presentation in PDF format, so that users of Adobe Acrobat or Adobe Reader can view it. Choose Export from the File tab to use this feature.

Save a presentation to your SkyDrive

1 On the ribbon, click the File tab to display the Backstage view and then select the Save As tab.

2 Click your SkyDrive.

3 In the Recent folders section, click one of the folders or click Browse.

The Save As dialog box opens.

4 If needed, select a different drive or folder.

5 Enter a file name for the presentation.

6 Click Save.

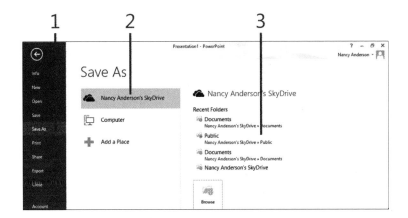

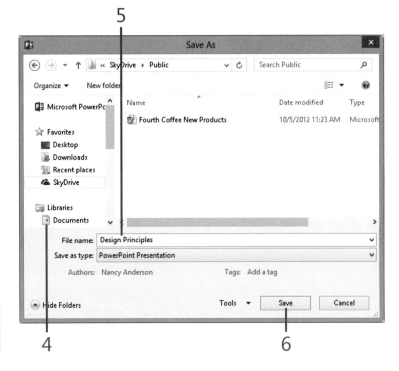

TIP Files saved to your local SkyDrive folders sync automatically with the online SkyDrive folders.

Closing a PowerPoint presentation

Close a file after you save it and finish working on it. This ensures that you won't make any inadvertent changes to the file. It also ensures that the computer will shut down more quickly when you finish working; you won't need to respond to any prompts about saving changes to files.

Close a Presentation

1   On the Quick Access Toolbar, click the Save button to be sure that all changes have been saved.

2   Click the Close button to close both the file and PowerPoint.

TRY THIS!   If you want to close an open presentation without closing PowerPoint—for example, to begin a new blank presentation—in the Backstage view, choose Close.

Working with slide masters

5

One of the hallmarks of a good presentation is a uniform look and feel. To achieve that consistency, you can use themes and color schemes built right into Microsoft PowerPoint 2013. (For more about these features, see Section 9, "Adjusting slide appearance," starting on page 117.) But, you might want to use other elements consistently from slide to slide, such as a company logo, and having to add these elements again and again—slide by slide—can be cumbersome.

That's where masters come in. Using a master, you can add a graphic, modify the text formatting or slide layout, or add a global footer. Then, whatever you add to the master appears on every slide.

Masters are flexible, as well. If you want one section of your presentation to use a master element or two, but in another section you want to introduce a change, you can use more than one master in your presentation to do so.

You can work with three types of masters in PowerPoint: a slide master, a handout master, and a notes master. Keep in mind that any changes you make to individual slides override the settings on masters.

In this section:

- Understanding how slide masters work
- Displaying and navigating the slide master
- Making changes to a slide master
- Changing master graphics and background
- Renaming and deleting slide layouts
- Inserting and removing slide masters
- Working with the handout master
- Working with the notes master

Understanding how slide masters work

Slide masters start out with a set of slide layouts defined by the currently applied theme. That theme determines the font treatment, placement and size of placeholders, background graphics, animation, and color scheme. You can make changes to any of the layouts in a slide master so that any time you apply one of those layouts to a slide, whatever is on that layout in the master appears automatically on the slides to which its applied. You can use the Edit Master tools on the Slide Master tab to add a master set or add a new layout to an existing master set. Use Edit Theme tools on the Slide Master tab to change formatting for the text on your slides.

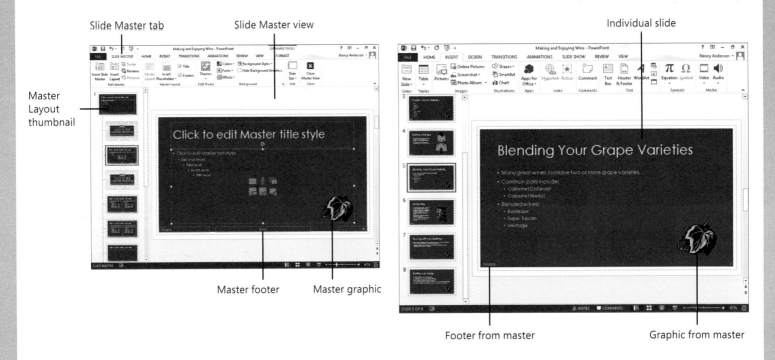

Slide Master tab

Slide Master view

Individual slide

Master Layout thumbnail

Master footer

Master graphic

Footer from master

Graphic from master

Displaying and navigating the slide master

To work with the slide master, you must change to Slide Master view. Using this view, you can see the various individual layouts contained within the master in the left pane and select which layout to change.

Display and navigate masters

1 On the View tab, in the Master Views group, choose Slide Master.

2 Drag the vertical scrollbar on the left pane to view more layouts in the master.

3 Drag the divider between panes if you want to see more or less of either pane.

4 To close Slide Master view, click the Close Master View button or on the View tab, in the Presentation Views group, click the Normal, Slide Sorter, Notes Page, or Reading View button.

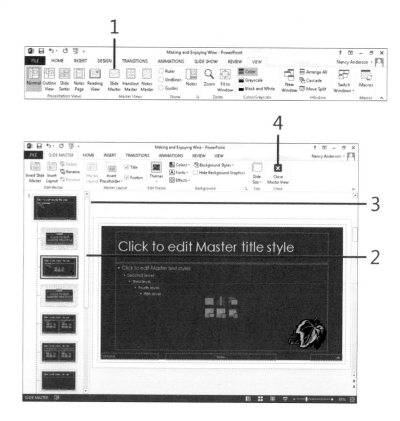

Making changes to a slide master

In Slide Master view, you can work with font formats and bullet list styles, insert text or text boxes, add graphics, or rearrange elements of any slide layout. (You learn more about how to take these actions in Section 6, "Building a presentation," Section 10, "Inserting media and drawing objects," and Section 9, "Adjusting slide appearance"). You make these changes much as you do in Normal view. However, any changes you make in Slide Master view are reflected on every slide to which the changed layout is applied. If you want to apply changes to all slides except the Title Slide layout, make those changes to the Master Layout at the top of the layout thumbnails. Two basic changes that you can start with are working with footer content and position, and adding another layout.

Insert footer information

1 With Slide Master view displayed, click in the center footer place-holder to select it. Note that the far-left and far-right placeholders are reserved for the current date and page number by default.

2 Enter whatever text you want in the placeholder.

3 If you want to move any of the three footer placeholder boxes, drag it to a new location on the slide.

4 To remove any of the three footer placeholder boxes, select it and press the Delete key.

> ✓ **TIP**   If you delete the left or right placeholder boxes with the date and page number, you can redisplay them by selecting the Footers check box in the Master Layout group on the Slide Master tab. The codes for the date and page number might not reappear with this method, however. If that's the case, you can instead copy (Ctrl+C) the applicable footer placeholder from another layout in the master and paste it (Ctrl+V) where needed.

> ✓ **TIP**   Rather than delete the date and page number placeholders, go to the Slide tab in the Header And Footer dialog box to control their display. To learn more, see "Insert headers or footers" on page 242 in Section 15, "Printing a presentation."

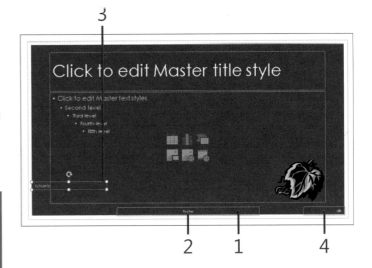

Add a layout

1 With Slide Master view displayed, on the Slide Master tab, in the Edit Master group, click Insert Layout.

2 On the new Custom Layout slide that appears, make any changes that you want to the layout, such as the following:

- On the Slide Master tab, in the Edit Master group, click Insert Placeholder and then click a choice on the menu to insert a new placeholder for any type of content.

- Add graphics or change placeholder text formatting.

- Move or delete placeholders as desired.

1

2

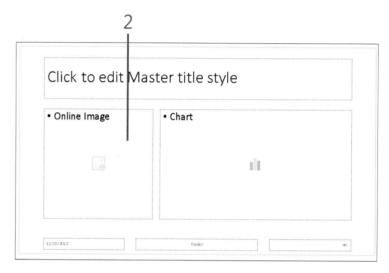

TRY THIS! You can quickly and easily remove the title or footer placeholders from a layout. On the Slide Master tab, in the Master Layout group, just clear the Title or Footers check box. The item you clear disappears from the current layout.

TIP If you want to include or exclude an item from all slide layouts, use the Master Layout. Click the Master Layout thumbnail to display it, and then on the Slide Master tab, click the Master Layout button. In the Master Layout dialog box, select or clear the desired check boxes to display or remove items such as a title or slide number from all slides and then click OK.

Changing the background and master graphics

In addition to working with the placeholders on a layout, you can add and format graphics, and change the background. Changes appear on every slide in the presentation that are based on that layout. Or, if you want the graphics or background changes to apply to all slides in the presentation, select the Master Layout thumbnail at the top of the pane, and make your changes.

Work with master graphics

1 In Slide Master view, select the layout on which you want to place the graphic (for example, the title slide or a content slide).

   If you want to insert the graphic on every layout except the Title Slide layout, click the top Master Layout thumbnail.

2 Click the Insert tab.

3 Use the controls in the Illustrations or Images group to insert a master graphic in your presentation:

   • Click to insert a picture or clip art

   • Click to insert a chart

(continued on next page)

Work with master graphics *(continued)*

4 When you have inserted a graphic on the slide master, you can resize it or drag it to wherever you want to position it.

SEE ALSO For more about inserting pictures, clip art, and charts in your presentation, see Section 10, "Inserting media and drawing objects," starting on page 127; for more about changing the size of objects, see "Resize objects" on page 176.

CAUTION When you place a master graphic, you typically put it in a corner of a slide so that it doesn't overlap placeholder text or elements such as large tables. Still, if you use a graphic on every slide, the odds are that it will overlap some object on a few slides in the presentation. Be sure to watch out for this. If it does occur, you can move the graphic or use the procedure in the task "Change the background color and hide graphics" on page 124 to remove the background graphic on the affected slides.

Change the master background

1 In Slide Master view, select the layout for which you want to change the background.

If you want to change the background on every layout except the Title Slide layout, click the top Master Layout thumbnail.

2 In the Slide pane, right-click the layout and then, on the shortcut menu that appears, click Format Background.

The Format Background pane opens.

3 Use the various choices to set the background formatting that you want.

4 Click the Close (X) button to close the pane and apply your changes.

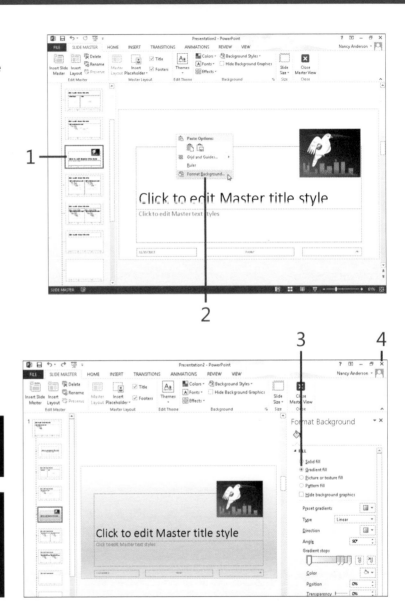

TRY THIS! In the Format Background pane, choose background settings and then click Apply To All (at the bottom) to apply the background formatting to all the layouts in the slide master.

TRY THIS! You can apply another theme to a layout. In Slide Master view, in the Thumbnails pane on the left, select a layout. On the Slide Master tab, in the Edit Theme group, click the Themes button. Right-click the theme that you want to apply to the selected layout and then, on the shortcut menu that appears, click Apply To Selected Slide Master.

Renaming and deleting slide layouts

When you create a new layout, you should give it a name to distinguish it from the other available layouts. Then, when you're adding a new slide or changing the layout for a slide in the presentation, you can be sure that you're choosing the right layout. If you have no more need for a layout, you can delete it to streamline the slide master.

Rename a layout

1 In Slide Master view, in the Thumbnails pane on the left, click the layout that you want to rename.

2 On the Slide Master tab, in the Edit Master group, click Rename.

The Rename Layout dialog box opens.

3 Type a new name for the layout.

4 Click Rename.

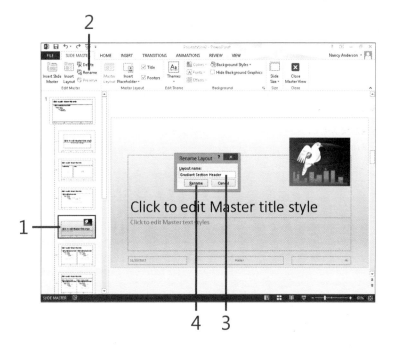

Delete a Layout

1 In Slide Master view, in the Thumbnails pane on the left, click the layout that you want to delete.

2 On the Slide Master tab, in the Edit Master group, click Delete.

PowerPoint removes the layout from the slide master.

> ⚠️ **CAUTION**   If you delete a layout from the slide master, you can't undo the delete; you must re-create the layout again. To avoid this problem, right-click a layout in the Thumbnails pane and then, on the shortcut menu that appears, click Duplicate Layout. Now, you can edit the duplicate and delete it if you no longer need it, leaving the original intact. Note that you cannot delete the Title Slide layout.

Inserting and removing slide masters

You can apply multiple themes to a single presentation in PowerPoint 2013. A set of master layouts is created whenever you apply another theme to some of your slides in the presentation, and another set of thumbnails is displayed in the Thumbnails pane of the Slide Master view. You can insert a new blank master that you can customize by using the Insert Slide Master command in the Edit Master group on the Slide Master tab. You also can insert another theme (and master for it) by using the Themes button in the Edit Theme group on the Slide Master tab.

Insert additional masters

1 In Slide Master view, click the Slide Master tab and then, in the Edit Master group, click Insert Slide Master.

2 To insert an additional theme in your presentation, in the Edit Theme group, click Themes. In the gallery that opens, click the theme that you want to apply.

> ⚠️ **CAUTION** Don't overdo it! The point of themes is that they instantly apply a consistent look and feel to your presentation. Mixing and matching too many themes creates a messy and cluttered-looking presentation. A couple of themes is typically the most you should use in any presentation to designate major sections or changes of mood.

> ✓ **TIP** You can also apply a theme to your presentation or to some of the slides in your presentation in Normal view. That theme is automatically added as a new set of masters in Slide Master view.

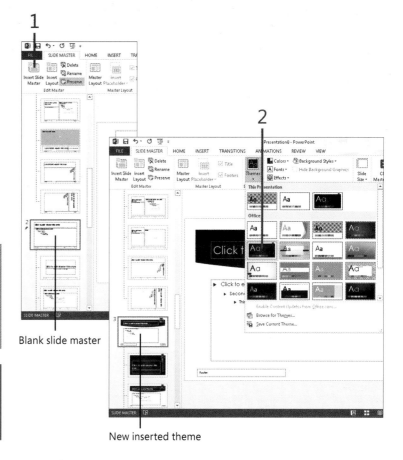

Blank slide master

New inserted theme

Delete additional masters

1 In Slide Master view, right-click the master layout thumbnail in the left pane that you want to delete. A shortcut menu appears.

2 Click Delete Master.

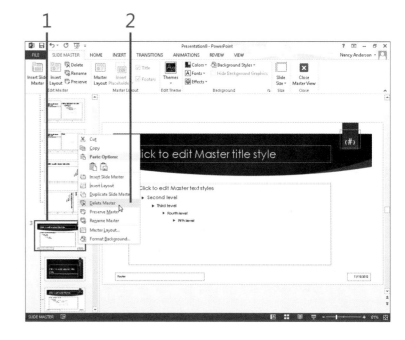

Working with the handout master

Handouts are essentially a printing option for PowerPoint 2013. You can print one, two, three, four, six, or nine slides on a page and provide those pages to your audience to follow along with your presentation or to take with them as a reminder of key points. In the Handout Master view, you can enter up to two headers and two footers, rearrange or delete placeholders, set the orientation of the handouts, and set the number of slides to print on a page.

Work with the Handout Master

1 On the View tab, in the Master Views group, click Handout Master.

2 Do any of the following:

- Click in a footer or header placeholder and enter text or replace the date or slide number element that's already there.

- Drag a footer or header placeholder to a new location.

- Click to remove any of the four footer or header placeholders from handouts.

3 Click the Handout Master contextual tab, click Slide Orientation or Handout Orientation, and then choose Portrait or Landscape.

(continued on next page)

> **TRY THIS!**   You can use the Insert tab when in Handout Master view to insert graphics that appear only on your handouts. For example, you might want to insert a logo along with the words "Company Confidential" on handouts to ensure that people treat the handouts as private.

Work with the Handout Master *(continued)*

4 In the Page Setup group, click Slides Per Page and then choose an option from the gallery.

5 In the Background group, click Background Styles and choose a background for the handouts from the gallery.

6 Again, in the Background group, click the Colors, Fonts, or Effects tool to choose formatting options from the various galleries.

7 When you're done configuring the handout master settings, click Close Master View to return to Normal view.

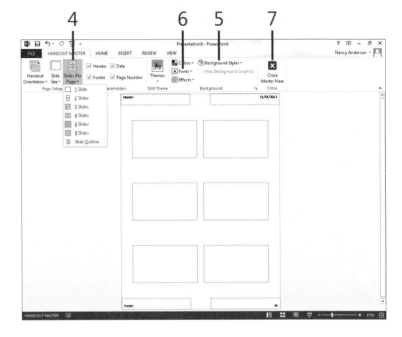

> **TIP** To omit background graphics from handouts that appear on the slides themselves (which can make the text easier to read), on the Handout Master tab, in the Background group, select the Hide Background Graphics check box.

Working with the notes master

In PowerPoint 2013, you can print handy reference notes for the benefit of the person who is making the presentation. Notes consist of a slide along with an area for notes and placeholders for header and footer text. You can enter notes in the Notes pane of Normal view. Using the notes master, you can arrange the placement of the various elements on the Notes page globally.

Work with notes master

1 On the View tab, in the Master Views group, click Notes Master.

2 Click in a footer or header placeholder and enter text or replace the date or slide number element that's already there.

3 Drag a footer or header placeholder to a new location.

4 Clear check boxes in the Placeholders group to remove any of the six placeholders from handouts.

5 In the Page Setup group, click Notes Page Orientation and choose Portrait or Landscape.

(continued on next page)

TIP   Be sure to format the notes body so that you can easily read your notes while making a presentation, which often take place in a darkened room. Make the font size large, and use a font that is clean and easy to read.

Work with notes master *(continued)*

6 Click the Background Styles down-arrow to open the Background Styles gallery and then click to choose a background for the handouts.

7 Click Close Master View when you're done with notes master settings to return to Normal view.

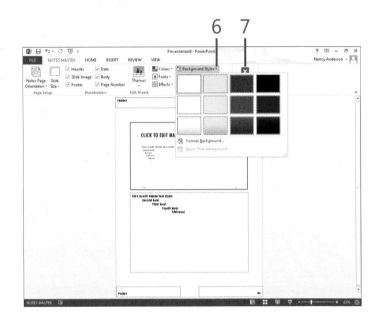

SEE ALSO For more information about formatting text to make it easily readable, see "Formatting text" on page 168.

Building a presentation

6

Although a presentation can contain text, graphics, animations, and special elements such as charts and WordArt, most presentations begin with you entering some kind of text. Text is used for the major headings for each slide as well as for the individual bullet points that provide the details of your topic. With Microsoft PowerPoint 2013, you can enter text in an outline or in placeholders on individual slides in Normal view. (For more about entering text in an outline, see Section 7, "Building a presentation outline," starting on page 97.)

In this section, you'll discover how to insert a new slide in your presentation and enter text in it. After you enter text, you often need to edit it by cutting or copying text and then pasting it in new locations, or finding and replacing text. Also in this section, you'll learn how to undo and redo actions as you go, which is useful if you change your mind as you build the content of your presentation.

You'll work with applying overall formatting to the placeholders and aligning the text within them. Finally, you'll learn about the Selection pane, which assists you in selecting and controlling placeholders on slides.

In this section:

- Understanding how to build a presentation
- Adding a slide
- Building slide content
- Adding special content
- Working with text
- Making text corrections
- Selecting placeholders
- Changing placeholder formatting

Understanding how to build a presentation

You enter most text, as well as elements such as pictures and tables, by using placeholders on slides in Normal view. You can format placeholders to use fill colors and borders. Slide title and subtitle placeholders typically hold a single heading, whereas content placeholders are used to enter a bulleted list of key points. When you enter text in placeholders, it is reflected in the Outline tab in Normal view.

New Slide button

Placeholder with centered text

Slide title placeholder (main topic)

Slide content placeholder (detailed topics)

Placeholder with fill color

TRY THIS! As with the Title Slide layout, the Section Header and Title Only layouts accept only text. Use the Blank layout to include whatever content you desire. Try inserting a Section Header or a Two Content slide layout from the New Slide button's gallery. You can add text to a blank slide by using a text box (see "Add a text box" on page 163), but remember that text in a text box is not reflected in the presentation outline.

SEE ALSO Although this section deals with the basics of inserting slides with a few different layouts, you learn about different slide layouts in more detail in Section 9, "Adjusting slide appearance," starting on page 117.

Adding a slide

When you open a blank presentation, PowerPoint 2013 provides you with one blank title slide. A title slide contains two placeholders—a title and a subtitle. When you insert another slide, a slide that uses the Title and Content layout is inserted by default. This layout contains a title placeholder in which you enter the topic for the slide, and a placeholder for inserting bulleted points for that topic or other types of content such as

a chart. Other slide layouts also use text placeholders, but title slides and title-and-content slides are the two types of you use most often for building presentation contents. (See Section 10, "Inserting media and drawing objects," starting on page 127, for information about working with slide layouts that include graphic elements.)

Insert a new slide

1 On the ribbon, click the Home tab.

2 In the Slides group, click New Slide to insert a new Title and Content slide.

3 Click the New Slide down-arrow.

The Office Theme gallery opens.

4 Click a layout in gallery.

With this method, you can choose any layout you want as you're creating the new slide.

1

2

3 4

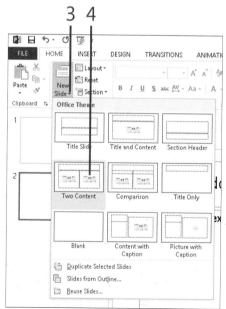

> ✓ **TIP** When you insert a new slide, it uses the layout of the slide that's selected when you click the New Slide button, except when you have a title slide displayed. PowerPoint 2013 assumes that you want only one title slide for your presentation, so when you display a title slide and click New Slide, the new slide uses the Title and Content layout.

Building slide content

After you have inserted a new slide and selected its layout, if desired, you can begin entering the text on a slide-by-slide basis in Normal view. To work with a previously created slide, in the Thumbnails pane at the left side of the view, click the corresponding thumbnail. When a placeholder is blank—that is, it displays only example text such as Click To Add Title—you can

click in the placeholder and begin typing. A fast way to add text to a placeholder is to copy and paste it from another slide or presentation. If a placeholder already has text that you entered previously, you might need to edit the text as described in "Edit text" on page 89, later in this section.

Enter text on slides

1 Click a title placeholder.

2 Type your text and then click anywhere outside the placeholder.

3 Click a content placeholder, type one line of text, and then press Enter. Repeat the process to add more lines of text.

PowerPoint adds bullets automatically if called for by the slide master for the theme applied to the presentation.

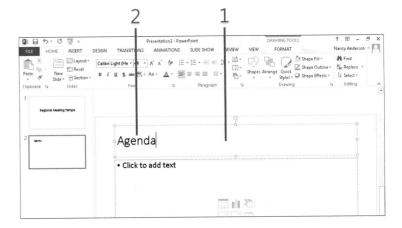

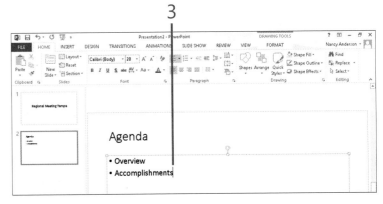

 TIP You can modify bullet point styles that are inserted in content placeholders. To do so, on the Home tab, in the Paragraph group, click the down-arrow on the Bullets button and then, in the gallery that opens, choose a different style or click Bullets And Numbering at the bottom of the gallery to customize bullet styles.

SEE ALSO For information about formatting the text you type into placeholders, see "Formatting text" on page 168.

Cut, copy, and paste text

1 Click the placeholder that you want to copy, or drag to select text within the placeholder if you want to copy or cut and paste the text only (and not the placeholder).

2 On the ribbon, click the Home tab.

3 In the Clipboard group, click Cut or Copy.

4 Click where you want to paste the text that is on the clipboard.

5 Click Paste.

The Paste Options button appears after you paste. You can press Esc to dismiss it if you don't need to select any of its formatting choices.

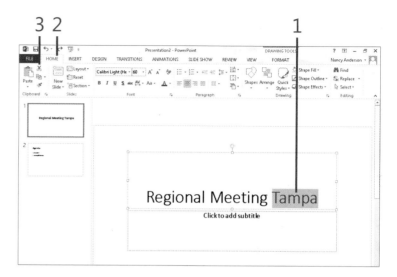

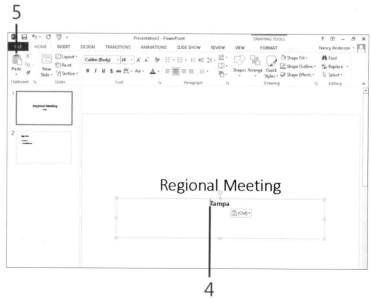

> **TIP** If you click the down-arrow on the Paste Options button, you can choose to keep the original formatting of the pasted text, use the destination formatting, or paste the text in a special format.

> **TRY THIS!** You are not limited to cutting or copying and pasting text on the same slide. You can cut or copy text from another slide in the same presentation or even another presentation file. You can then paste it into any destination slide you want. Use the Windows taskbar or the Switch Windows button in the Window group on the View tab to move between open presentation files.

Adding special content

Text placeholders can hold a few other types of content beyond formatted text. You can insert symbols from the Symbol dialog box at any location within text. You might want to do this for practical reasons, such as to insert the Euro (€) currency symbol before a currency value, to insert a fraction character, or to insert a special mark such as the trademark (™) symbol. Or, you can insert fanciful symbols to decorate text. With PowerPoint 2013, you can insert another type of special content—a preformatted date that can be set to update to the current date automatically every time you open the presentation file.

Insert a symbol

1 Click in a placeholder at the point at which you want to insert a symbol.

2 On the ribbon, click the Insert tab.

3 In the Symbols group, click Symbol.

The Symbol dialog box opens.

(continued on next page)

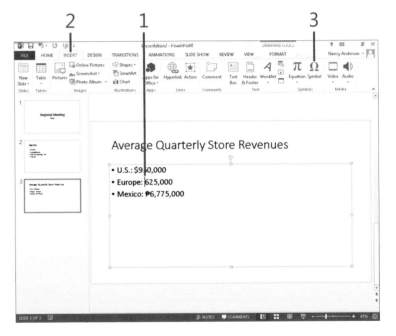

Insert a symbol *(continued)*

4 Click the down-arrow adjacent to the Font text box and then click a font to select it.

5 Scroll to locate the symbol that you want to insert and then click the symbol.

6 Click Insert.

The symbol is inserted on the slide at the point in the text where you clicked.

7 Continue to locate and insert the symbols that you need. Click the Close button on the dialog box when you're done.

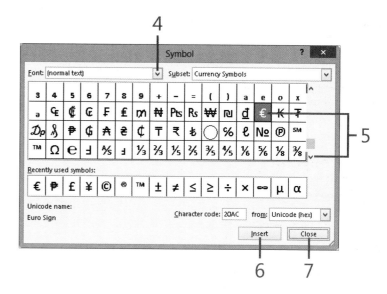

> **TIP** All fonts have some symbols, such as percent and dollar signs, but if you're looking for little pictures or design elements rather than text, your best bet is to choose one of these fonts: Symbol, Wingdings, Wingdings 2 or 3, or Webdings.

> **TRY THIS!** For some fonts, you can narrow available choices in the Symbols dialog box by choosing a category from the Subset list. For example, if you want symbols only for international currencies, choose the Currency Symbols category, and if you want only arrow symbols, choose Arrows.

Insert the date and time

1 Click at the spot in the placeholder where you want to insert the date and time.

2 On the ribbon, click the Insert tab.

3 In the Text group, click Date & Time.

The Date And Time dialog box opens.

4 In the Available Formats list, click a date and time format.

5 To have the date change to the current date when you open the file, select the Update Automatically check box.

6 Click OK.

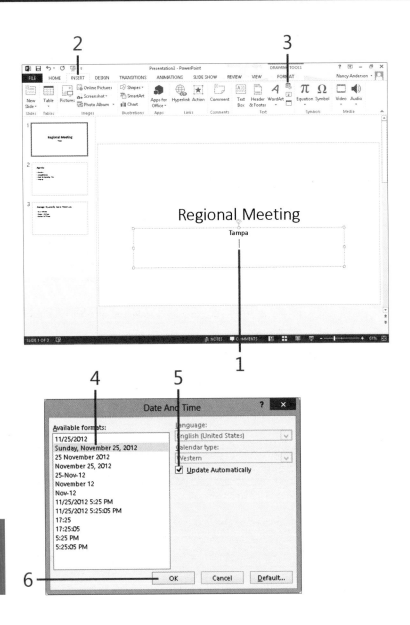

Working with text

Most of us aren't perfect and seldom get everything exactly right upon the first draft when we're writing. We need to go back and make changes and even undo some things we've done. To help out with these tasks, PowerPoint 2013 makes it easy to edit text and undo or redo actions.

Edit text

1 Click in a placeholder at a location where you want to begin your edit. (If you select text to edit it, the mini toolbar appears, which offers some common formatting tools.)

2 Take any of the following actions:

- Press Delete to remove text to the right of the cursor, one character at a time.

- Press Backspace to remove text to the left of the cursor, one character at a time.

- Drag over text and then press the Delete key to delete all of the selected text at once.

- Begin typing any additional or replacement text.

3 Click outside the placeholder.

> **SEE ALSO** For information about cutting, copying, and pasting entire slides or duplicating slide contents, see "Managing slides in Slide Sorter view" on page 110.

> **TIP** You can also edit text in Outline view. Remember that any change you make to placeholder text on a slide is reflected in the outline, and vice versa. See Section 7, starting on page 97, for more about working with a presentation outline.

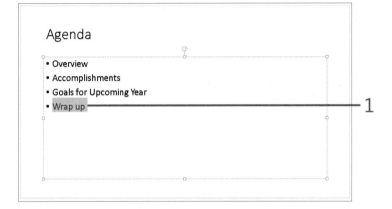

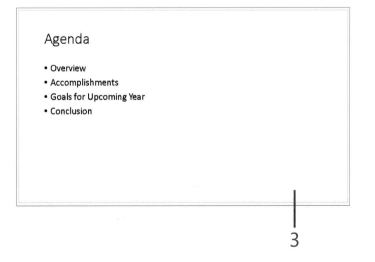

Undo and redo an action

1 After performing an action such as typing, formatting, or moving an object, on the Quick Access Toolbar, click the Undo [Action] button.

The previous action is reversed.

2 To redo an undone action, on the Quick Access Toolbar, click the Redo [Action] button.

3 If you want to undo a series of actions, click the arrow on the Undo [Action] button and then, in the list that appears, choose the actions that you want to discard.

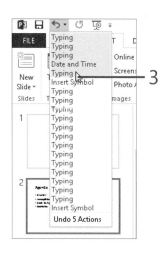

 CAUTION You can't undo an action you performed prior to other actions without undoing every action you performed following it. In this case, it might be simplest to just make the change yourself by retyping, reformatting, or redoing whatever it was you did that you want undone.

TIP A quick and easy way to undo what you just did is to press Ctrl+Z. To redo what you've undone, press Ctrl+Y.

Making text corrections

Sometimes when you create a presentation, you need to change every instance of a word or phrase. For example, perhaps your company has changed the name of a product under development after you completed your presentation, referring to the product by its original name. Finding and editing each instance of the name manually can be time-consuming. Instead, you can use the Find And Replace feature in PowerPoint 2013 to easily find every instance and change them all at once or one by one. Also, when PowerPoint encounters a word that is not in its dictionary, it flags the word as a potential typographical error by using a red wavy underline. You can correct such errors by right-clicking the underlined word and clicking the preferred correction from those offered by PowerPoint.

Find and replace text

1 Display slide 1 of the presentation and then, on the ribbon, click the Home tab.

2 In the Editing Group, click Replace.

   The Replace dialog box opens.

3 In the Find What text box, enter a word or phrase that you want to locate.

4 In the Replace With text box, enter the replacement word or phrase.

5 Click Find Next.

   PowerPoint finds and flags the first match occurrence that matches the contents of the Find What text box.

6 Do one of the following:

   • Click Find Next to find the next instance of the text.

   • Click Replace to replace the currently selected instance of the text.

   • Click Replace All to replace all instances of the text. Note that you are not asked to confirm this choice, but you can use the Undo action to revert changes if anything disastrous happens.

   (continued on next page)

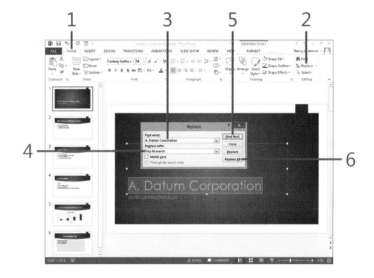

Find and replace text *(continued)*

7 When you finish finding or replacing text, PowerPoint displays a confirming message. Click OK, and then click Close to dismiss the Replace dialog box.

> ✓ **TIP** Select the Match Case and Find Whole Words Only check boxes in the Replace dialog box to narrow your search. If, for instance, you want to find the word Bell (a last name) but you don't want lowercase instances of the word bell or words such as bellow, you could use both of these qualifiers in your find and replace operation.

Correct Obvious Typographical Errors

1 Click the Next and Previous buttons at the bottom of the slider bar to move through the presentation and review the contents of various slides.

2 When you see a word with a red wavy underline, right-click the word.

3 On the options menu that appears, click the desired replacement.

> 🔍 **SEE ALSO** You will learn how to perform a full spelling check in Section 13, "Finalizing your slide show," starting on page 207.

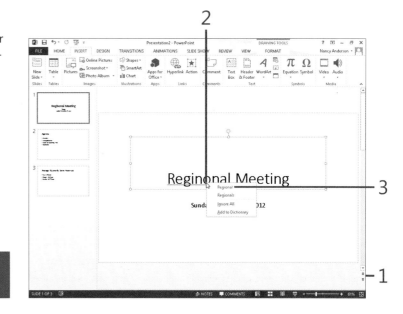

Selecting Placeholders

With the exception of text boxes (covered on page 163 in Section 10), placeholders are where you create the elements of your presentation in PowerPoint 2013. They contain text, drawings, pictures, charts, and more. Placeholders provide an easy way to arrange the components of each slide, and because they come with certain predesigned formatting, they make adding everything from a bulleted list to a chart easy. By selecting a placeholder (made easier with the Selection pane), you can align the contents of placeholders and format their text, backgrounds, and borders.

Use the Selection pane

1 In Normal view, click on a slide in the Slide pane.

2 Click the Home tab.

3 In the Editing group, click Select.

4 In the drop-down list that appears, click Selection Pane.

The Selection pane opens. Each item listed in the pane corresponds to an object on the current slide.

(continued on next page)

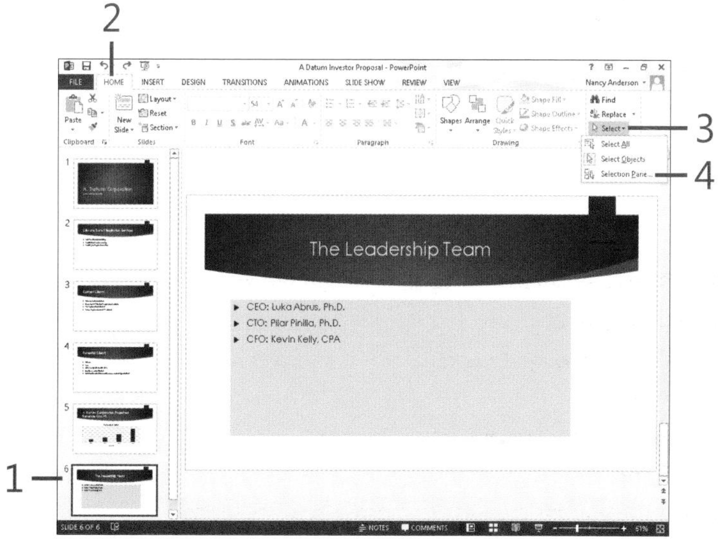

TIP In addition to using the Selection pane to help you select objects, on the Home tab, you can click the Arrange button and use the Bring To Front and Send To Back buttons to move a selected object in a stack of objects in front of or behind other objects.

Use the Selection pane *(continued)*

5 In the Selection pane, do any of the following:

- Click an item in the list to select the object on the slide.
- Click Hide All to hide all objects on the slide.
- Click Show All to redisplay all objects on the slide.
- Click the Visibility button for an item to show or hide that individual object on the slide.

6 When you finish using the Selection pane, click the Close button to exit the pane.

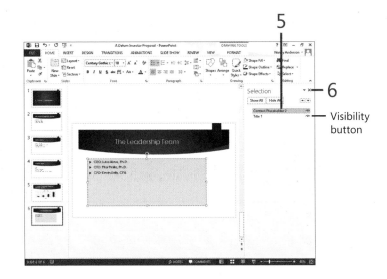

TIP If you click an item in the Selection pane, the Format contextual tab appears on the ribbon. This tab also contains the Arrange group of tools, including the Selection Pane, Bring To Front, and Send To Back buttons.

SEE ALSO For more information about working with objects on your slides, see Section 10, starting on page 127.

Changing placeholder formatting

If you select the placeholder overall, such as by using the Selection pane, you can update the formatting of the placeholder and its contents. For example, you can change the alignment of the text in the placeholder, add a border to it, and apply a fill. Try a couple of placeholder formatting example tasks now.

Align placeholder contents

1 Click the placeholder containing the text that you want to align.

2 If you want to align only one line among several, select that specific text within the placeholder.

3 On the Home tab, in the Paragraph Group, click the desired alignment button.

The text aligns accordingly.

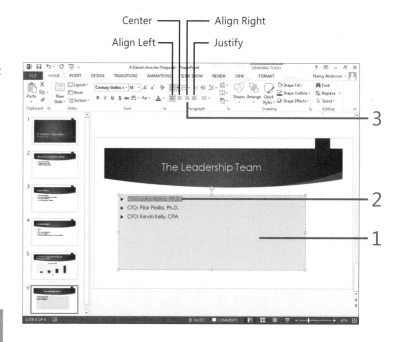

✓ **TIP** Use centered text for emphasis for a single line of text. If you're working with bulleted lists, you should usually use left or justified alignment so that each bulleted item begins at the same place, making the list easier to follow.

Format placeholders

1 Right-click the placeholder border and then, on the shortcut menu that appears, choose Format Shape.

The Format Picture pane opens. Note that you also could use the Style, Fill, or Outline buttons that appear rather than Format Shape.

2 In the Format Picture pane, click Fill.

Note that you would click Line, instead, to expand the line options or one of the other category icons near the top of the pane to find other formatting settings.

3 To adjust the fill or other formatting, use the settings that appear. Whatever settings you make are previewed on the placeholder.

4 Click the Close button in the Format Picture pane to apply your new settings.

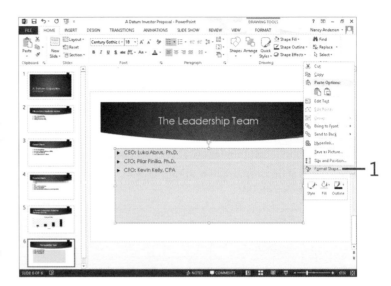

> ⚠ **CAUTION** Don't go overboard adding effects to placeholders, especially if your slide contains a lot of graphics and text. Let the text be the important element on any slide to ensure that your message comes across.

> ✓ **TIP** After you apply a fill color to a placeholder, a quick way to change that color is to select the placeholder, click the Shape Fill button on the Drawing Tools|Format contextual tab, and then choose a new color.

Building a presentation outline

7

Microsoft PowerPoint users have had the capability to create a slide show by entering an outline for quite some time now. In PowerPoint 2013, this feature now resides in a separate view called Outline view. An outline breaks down information into multiple headings and subheading levels. You can use Outline view in PowerPoint to enter text, reorganize it into topics and subtopics, and reorder the contents of your presentation.

Because it can be faster to enter text in Outline view rather than on individual slides, using it saves time when you are creating a text heavy presentation. After creating the outline, you can resume working in Normal view to adjust the look of individual slides.

To access Outline view, on the View tab, in the Presentation Views group, click the Outline View button. When you enter text on a slide, PowerPoint adds the content to the outline, and vice versa. As you work in the outline, the slide that corresponds to the text you're working on appears in the Slide pane, so you can see how changes to the outline affect the slide. Another nice aspect of Outline view in PowerPoint is that you can cut and paste or directly import an outline you create in a Microsoft Word document into the presentation.

In this section:

- Understanding the relationship of the outline to slides
- Working with the outline
- Adding text in the outline pane
- Viewing and rearranging outline contents
- Working with outline contents

Understanding the relationship of the outline to slides

Different slide layouts contain different placeholders, such as for the title, subtitle, text, and content. You can enter text in the placeholders on a slide in the Slide pane or within the outline in the Outline pane of Outline view.

When you enter text into title, subtitle, or text placeholders in the Slide pane, the text also appears in the outline. When you enter a top-level heading in the outline, PowerPoint creates a new slide, and that heading appears in the slide

title placeholder. Any text that you enter at an indented level in the Outline pane becomes a bullet point in a content placeholder on the slide. On a title slide, the indented text becomes the subtitle.

Graphics do not appear in the outline. Text in text boxes, WordArt, and SmartArt graphics (all are drawing objects that are different from text or content placeholders) also don't appear in the outline.

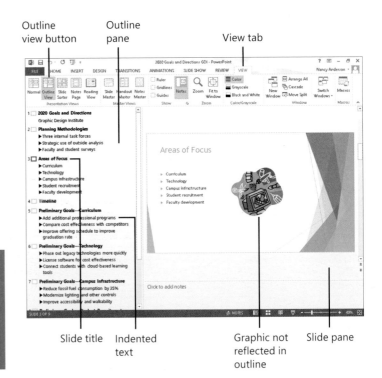

Outline view button

Outline pane

View tab

Slide title Indented text Graphic not reflected in outline Slide pane

TIP If your bullet points are long and you need to see more in the outline text, you can drag the border at the right side of the Outline pane to the right to make it wider. You can also change the zoom of the text in the pane. To do so, click in the Outline pane, click the View tab, and then in the Zoom group, click the Zoom button. In the Zoom dialog box that opens, select the size option that you want and click OK.

Working with the outline

You can work on an outline in Outline view by using the Outline pane displayed at the left side of the view. With the Outline pane, you can compare the outline with slides in the Slide pane at right, which might show objects such as pictures, text boxes, shapes, and more that don't show up in the outline. Entering

text in the outline can be faster than entering it on individual slides, partly because you are focused purely on presentation text content. You can increase the size of the Outline pane to further focus on the outline text by dragging the divider between the panes to the right.

Display Outline view

1 Click the View tab.

2 Click the Outline View button to display the Outline view.

3 Drag the divider between the panes to change their relative sizes.

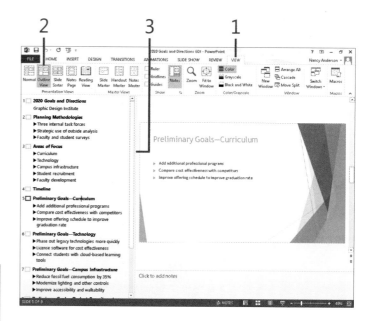

> **TRY THIS!** If you have a long presentation and you expand the Outline pane to view more of the outline, the slide preview can become too small to be readable. Select an item on the slide, and then in the lower-right corner of the PowerPoint window, drag the zoom slider to enlarge the slide preview but not the outline text.

> **TIP** You can change the text size and font in the Outline pane or the Slide pane. A change made in one pane is reflected in the other. For more information about changing text formatting, see "Formatting text" on page 168.

Adding text in the Outline pane

The Outline pane helps you to enter presentation text faster because you don't have to deal with placeholders or graphics. After you enter the title, adding text to the outline involves pressing Enter to create a new line in the outline and then typing the text, which appears at the same outline level as the line above it. You can then demote text to become a subheading (subtitle or bullet point) or promote a bullet point to become the next slide title.

Each line at the highest outline level is a slide title. If you build a presentation from the beginning in Outline view, PowerPoint automatically assigns the Title Slide layout to the first slide. A title slide comprises only a title and subtitle. When you add subsequent slides in the outline, PowerPoint assigns the Title And Content layout to them by default. You can then type and indent slide content and change the slide layout if needed.

Add a slide title

1   In Outline view, click in the Outline pane. If there is already text in the outline, click at the end of it, press Enter, and then press Shift+Tab as many times as needed to move the text to the top level until a slide icon appears.

2   Type some text, which is automatically formatted as a slide title, and press Enter.

The slide title appears in both the Outline and Slide panes, and the insertion point is in place to create the next slide title.

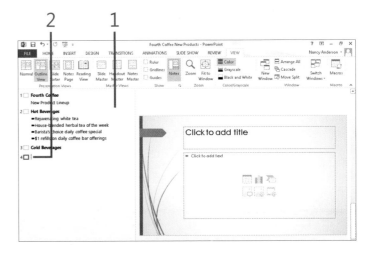

> **SEE ALSO**   For more information about slide layouts and how to change them, see "Understanding what slide layouts and themes control" on page 118 and "Applying a layout" on page 119.

> **TIP**   When the outline contains more slides than can be displayed in the Outline pane, a scroll bar appears along the right side of the pane. You can use it to scroll the outline up and down so that you can see and edit whatever slides in the outline need text changes.

Promote and demote outline text

1 Enter text in the Outline pane of Outline view or click in an existing line of text to select it.

2 Click the Home tab. In the Paragraph group, choose Increase List Level or press Tab.

Increase List Level demotes the heading. After you demote a heading to the bullet point level, pressing Enter creates the next heading at the same bullet point level.

3 To start the next slide, type a heading, and then on the Home tab, in the Paragraph group, choose Decrease List Level or press Shift+Tab. Both methods promote the heading to slide title level.

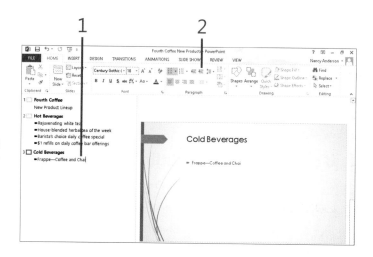

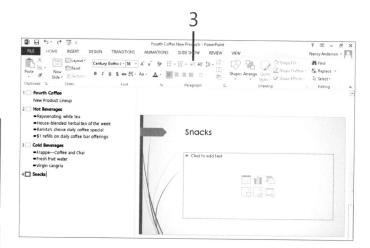

> **TIP** As a rule, two levels of bullets below the slide title is the most you should ever have. If you have that much detail to provide about a point, divide it among separate slides. Also, in the typical presentation environment, attendees can't possibly see more than two levels of headings on the screen.

> **TRY THIS!** In PowerPoint 2013, when you select text in the outline pane, a mini toolbar containing the most commonly used text formatting tools appears. You can use the Decrease List Level and Increase List Level buttons on the mini toolbar to structure your outline.

Viewing and rearranging outline contents

After you enter your presentation content and demote and promote headings to create an outline structure, you can work with the contents in various ways in Outline view. For example, at times you might want to view just the slide titles; at other times, you might prefer to see all the detailed headings. (Collapsing or expanding your outline has no effect on what appears in the Slide pane or on what appears when you give your slide presentation in Slide Show view.) You might also want to move headings around in an outline to reorganize the order of the slides.

Expand and collapse the outline

1 In Outline view, right-click a slide in the Outline pane.

2 Click Collapse and then do either of the following:

  - Choose Collapse to hide all the subheads for this slide title.

  - Choose Collapse All to hide all the subheads for the presentation.

3 Click Expand and then do either of the following to expand the outline:

  - Choose Expand to display all the subheads for this slide title.

  - Choose Expand All to display all subheads in the presentation.

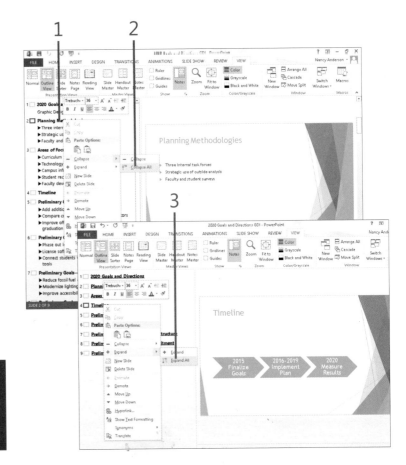

TRY THIS! In a longer presentation, collapse headings for slides on which you've finished working to make it easier to scroll through your outline to find information. When you are ready to view all your contents again, right-click in the Outline pane, choose Expand in the options menu that appears, and then click Expand All.

Move slides or text up and down in an outline

1 Right-click the line of text or drag to select multiple lines of text that you want to move.

2 In the shortcut menu that appears, choose Move Up or Move Down.

The selected line or lines move one line up or down, together.

3 To move an entire slide, you can drag the slide icon to a new position in the outline.

A horizontal line appears, indicating the position of the slide as you drag.

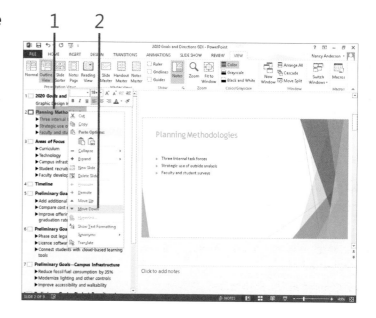

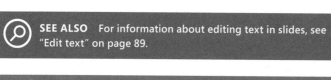

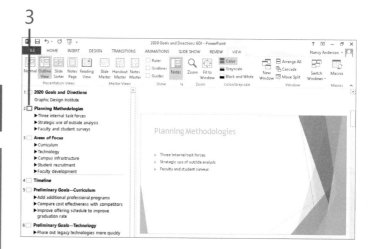

SEE ALSO   For information about editing text in slides, see "Edit text" on page 89.

TIP   If slide subheads are collapsed under the title and you move the title, all subheads move along with their slide title. If you don't want to move a subhead, you must first expand the slide and then either move the subhead to another family of headings (by cutting and pasting it elsewhere) or promote it to be a slide title on its own.

Working with outline contents

Text formatting appears by default in the Outline pane, but you can turn it off and back on easily. Turning off the formatting causes all of the text to be displayed using the Calibri Light font, no matter what theme you have applied. Removing any busier formatting that you have applied makes it easier for you to focus on the meaning of the words as you edit and review your slides.

Finally, instead of creating an outline, you can import any text you've created and outlined in a Word 2013 (or earlier version) file. In the Word document, apply heading styles to define the outline levels. For example, any text that uses the Heading 1 style in the Word document becomes a slide title in PowerPoint, Heading 2 text becomes slide bullets, and so on.

Turn formatting on and off in an outline

1 Right-click anywhere in the Outline pane.

2 In the shortcut menu, choose Show Text Formatting.

3 To hide text formatting, right-click in the Outline pane and choose Show Text Formatting again.

TIP Showing formatting in the outline is a good way to see whether you have a balance of fonts or formats (such as bold) in your presentation and to confirm that you have kept text formatting consistent overall. Another good way to view this is to display Slide Sorter view.

Insert a Word outline into PowerPoint

1 Press Ctrl+N to display a new, blank presentation.

2 Click the Home tab.

3 In the Slides Group, click the Slide button down arrow.

4 Click Slides From Outline.

5 In the Insert Outline dialog box, locate the Word document you want to use and click Insert. The outline content appears as slides in the blank presentation.

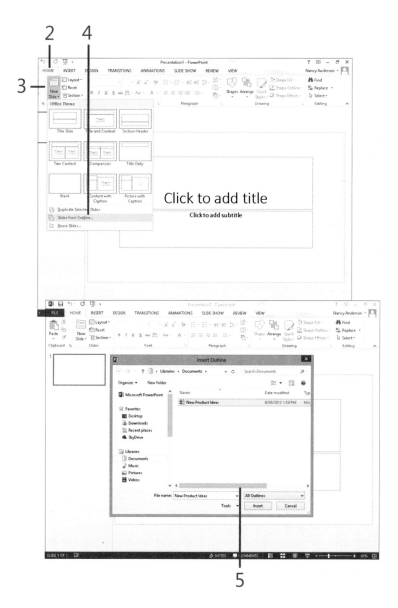

TIP You can also copy text from the PowerPoint Outline view Outline pane and paste it into Word to create a Word outline from it. You also can export the presentation outline to Word. Click the File tab, and click Export. Click Create Handouts under Export, and then click the Create Handouts button. In the Send to Microsoft Word dialog box, click the Outline only option button, and then click OK. No matter which method you use, you will have to reapply the outline levels once the presentation outline is in Word.

Managing and viewing slides

8

After you create slides, you often need to work with them to refine your content. For example, you might want to move among your slides to review their content, delete or copy certain slides, move slides, or hide them in the presentation. The Thumbnails pane in Normal view in Microsoft PowerPoint 2013 is useful for navigating the slides in your presentation; to see the larger view of the selected slide in the Slide pane, simply click its thumbnail.

Sometimes while refining a presentation, you need to delete a slide that's no longer relevant or copy and paste a slide from one place—or one presentation—into another. PowerPoint also has a handy feature to duplicate a slide. If the content of your presentation needs reorganizing, you can use Slide Sorter view to move slides around quickly and easily.

You can insert sections to break up larger presentations so that you can focus on the portion on which you want to work. Sections are displayed both in the Thumbnails pane in Normal view and in Slide Sorter view.

Finally, you can choose not to show certain slides while running your presentation by hiding them. You can easily unhide them when you need to use them again. Hiding and unhiding slides make it easy to customize presentations for different audiences.

In this section:

- Navigating slides in Normal view
- Deleting slides in Slide Sorter view
- Managing slides in Slide Sorter view
- Hiding and unhiding slides
- Working with sections

Navigating slides in Normal view

PowerPoint 2013 offers several views in which you can choose to work with your slides. In Normal view, the Slides pane is the central display area for the currently selected slide. Typically, this is where you focus on the design elements of each slide. In addition, the Thumbnails pane, which displays to the left of the Slides pane, shows all the slides in your presentation in the order in which they appear. The thumbnails in this pane give an overview of the look and contents of all slides in sequence, with the selected thumbnail's slide shown in more detail in the Slides pane to the right.

Display slides

1   Display the Thumbnails pane in Normal view. If it is collapsed, redisplay it by clicking the button above Thumbnails, in the bar at the left.

2   Using the Thumbnails pane scroll bar, do any of the following:

- Click the Scroll Down button to move ahead in the presentation.
- Click the Scroll Up button to move back in the presentation.
- Drag the large white box on the scroll bar to move ahead or back in the presentation by one or more slides at a time.
- Click just above or just below the scroll bar to move ahead or back in the presentation in increments equal to the number of slides that appear in the pane.

3   Click a slide to select it.

The slide is displayed in the Slide pane.

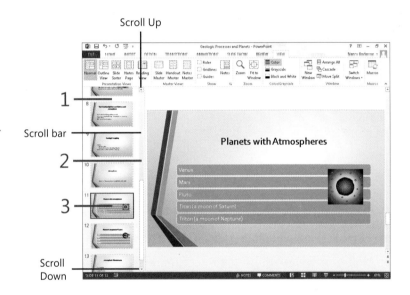

TIP   You also can use the scroll bar to the right of the Slide pane to navigate. Click the Scroll Up button to display the previous slide and the Scroll Down button to move to the next slide.

TIP   You can use the zoom slider in the lower-right corner of the PowerPoint window to enlarge and reduce the selected slide's contents in the Slides pane. (Click a blank area of the slide to ensure that the focus is in the Slides pane.) If you zoom out and enlarge the contents and then need more space to show the enlarged slide on your screen, you can shrink the Thumbnails pane by using the method just described in the Try This! tip.

Deleting slides in Slide Sorter view

As with anything you write, part of the process of building a PowerPoint 2013 presentation includes revising and refining your content as you go along. Just as you edit a report by deleting a sentence, you can delete a slide in a presentation to remove its content. Deleting a slide and performing other organizational tasks are simple in Slide Sorter view.

Delete slides

1. On the View tab, in the Presentation Views group, click the Slide Sorter button. The Slide Sorter view appears.

   You also can use the zoom slider in the lower-right corner to control how many thumbnails appear in the view.

2. Right-click a slide.

3. On the shortcut menu that appears, choose Delete Slide.

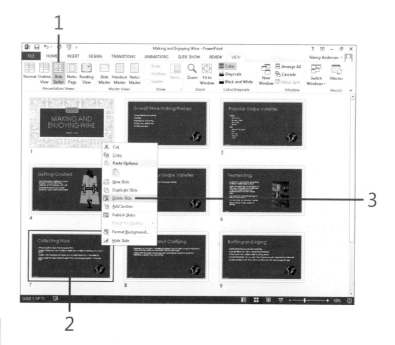

> ⚠ **CAUTION** If you delete a slide and exit PowerPoint, that slide is gone forever. Be sure that you don't need any of a slide's content before you delete it.

> 🔍 **SEE ALSO** Instead of deleting a slide, you can temporarily hide it from view. Then, if you decide you need the contents later, you can simply unhide it. See "Hiding and unhiding slides" on page 112 to learn about this feature.

Managing slides in Slide Sorter view

You can copy a slide so that you can base a new slide on existing content. It's also typical to rearrange the flow of your thoughts as you write. In PowerPoint 2013, that's as easy as moving a slide around in your presentation. As for deleting a slide, you can tackle that task in Slide Sorter view, as well.

Copy and paste slides

1   In Slide Sorter view, click the slide that you want to copy.

If you want to copy more than one contiguous slide, click the first slide, hold down Shift, and then click the last slide. To select non-contiguous slides, click the first one, hold down Ctrl, and then click additional slides to include them in the selection.

2   On the ribbon, click the Home tab.

3   In the Clipboard group, click the Copy button.

4   If necessary, create or switch to another presentation file and click the slide after which you want to paste the copied slides.

5   On the Home tab, click Paste.

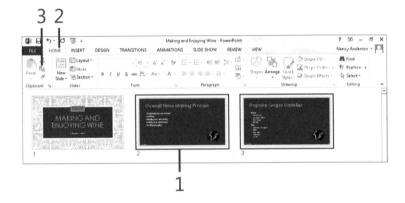

✓ **TIP** You can also use keyboard shortcuts to cut, copy, and paste selected slides. Keyboard shortcuts are by default displayed in the ScreenTip that appears when you hold your mouse pointer over an item on the ribbon. Use Ctrl+X to cut, Ctrl+C to copy, and Ctrl+V to paste.

🔍 **SEE ALSO** Use the procedures here to cut, copy, and paste entire slides. For more about cutting, copying, and pasting specific elements from within the contents of slides, see "Cut, copy, and paste text" on page 85.

Duplicate and move slides

1 In Slide Sorter view, right-click the slide that you want to duplicate.

2 On the shortcut menu that appears, click Duplicate Slide.

The duplicate slide appears to the right of the original slide.

3 Drag the slide to move it to where you want it to appear in the presentation.

A special mouse pointer appears and the thumbnail moves to indicate the new position.

4 Release the mouse button to place the slide in the new position.

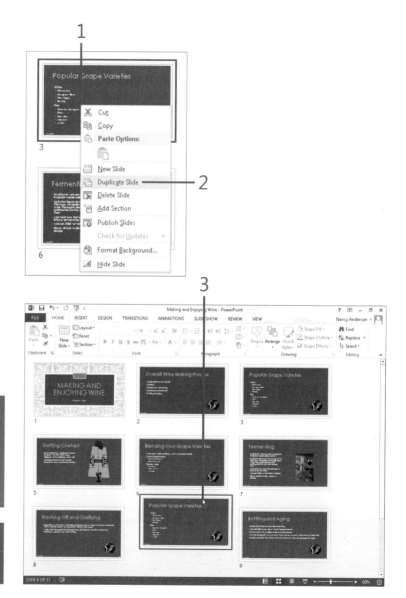

 TIP After you duplicate a slide, you can move the duplicate wherever you want in the presentation and make changes to it.

You can also cut, copy, paste, and duplicate slides by using the Thumbnails pane in Normal view. In the Thumbnails pane, just right-click any slide and choose the appropriate command from the shortcut menu that appears.

 SEE ALSO For more about managing slides in the Outline pane, see "Move slides or text up and down in an outline" on page 103.

Hiding and unhiding slides

Sometimes you might want to use a subset of slides for a presentation, or perhaps you need to hide a single slide because it contains information that's not appropriate for a particular audience. For example, you might choose not to show a management benefits slide when you're making a presentation about benefits to nonmanagers. In that case, you can easily hide the slide, give the presentation, and then unhide it later, when needed.

Hide slides

1 On the status bar, click the Slide Sorter view button.

   Or, on the View tab, in the Presentation Views group, click Slide Sorter.

2 Click a slide to select it.

   If you want to hide more than one contiguous slide, click the first slide, hold down Shift, and then click the last slide. To select noncontiguous slides, click the first one, hold down Ctrl, and then click additional slides to include them in the selection.

3 On the ribbon, click the Slide Show tab.

4 In the Set Up group, click Hide Slide to hide all selected slides.

   A gray slash (hidden slide mark) appears over the slide number indicating that it is hidden; the slide does not appear when you run the presentation.

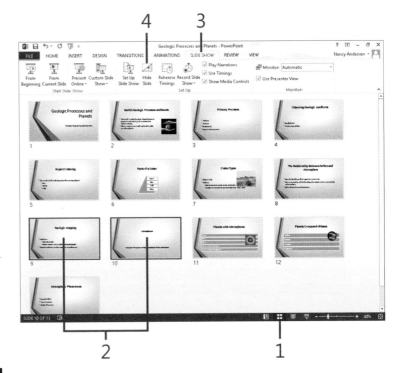

TRY THIS! Try printing a presentation that includes hidden slides. When you display the Print options in the Backstage view, you can open the Print All Slides drop-down list and ensure that the Print Hidden Slides option is selected so that slides you've hidden are included in the printout.

SEE ALSO For more information about printing presentations with hidden slides, see "Select the slides to print" on page 248.

Unhide slides

1 In Slide Sorter view, select the slide or slides that you want to unhide.

2 On the Slide Show tab, in the Set Up group, click Hide Slide.

The gray slash (hidden slide mark) disappears from the slide number. The slides now appear when you run the presentation.

Hidden
slide mark **2**

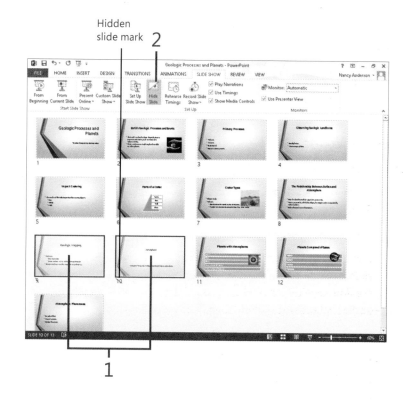

1

TRY THIS! Play the slide show before and after hiding slides to understand how hiding slides works. See Section 14, "Running a presentation," starting on page 225 to learn more.

Working with sections

Sections in PowerPoint 2013 help you find your way around large presentations. They function something like headings in a long report, making it easier to locate groups of slides that address similar topics. When you create a section and name it, its name appears in a bar separating the slides within the section from others in the presentation. You can use a feature on that bar to expand or collapse sections, which is useful for focusing on just one section at a time.

Add a section

1 On the status bar, click the Slide Sorter view button.

Or, on the View tab, in the Presentation Views group, click Slide Sorter.

2 Click the thumbnail for the slide that you want to be the first in the new section.

3 On the Home tab, in the Slides group, click Section and then choose Add Section.

4 Repeat steps 1 through 3 to create additional sections.

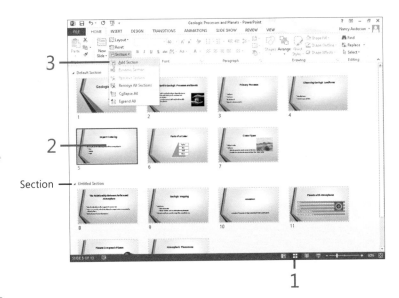

> **TRY THIS!**   Create several sections in your presentation, and then in Slide Sorter view click the small arrow to the left of a section's name to collapse it. Click the arrow again to expand that section. Experiment with using this feature to navigate through a large presentation.

> **TRY THIS!**   You can also rearrange sections in your presentation by choosing Move Section Up or Move Section Down from the shortcut menu that appears when you right-click a section.

Rename or delete a section

1 In Slide Sorter view, right-click a section name and then, on the shortcut menu that appears, click Rename Section.

The Rename Section dialog box opens.

2 Enter a new name.

3 Click Rename.

4 To delete a section, right-click a section name and then, on the shortcut menu that appears, choose Remove Section.

The section (but not the slides within it) disappears.

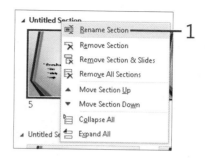

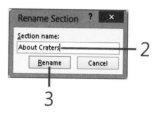

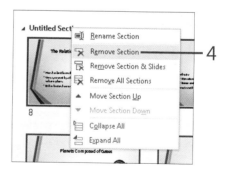

> **TIP** You can also work with sections from the Thumbnails pane in Normal view. To do so, right-click the section to work with the same shortcut menu displayed in step 3.

> **TIP** If you want to get rid of all your sections at some point, right–click a section and then choose Remove All Sections from the shortcut menu that appears. If you want to get rid of both a section and the slides within it, choose Remove Section & Slides.

Adjusting slide appearance

9

A presentation has to have solid content and clearly fleshed-out topics, but it must also hold your audience's attention. Visual enhancements such as color, font styles, and graphics go a long way toward impressing your audience through your professional approach.

For Microsoft PowerPoint 2013, you now have several built-in design elements that you can use for your presentations. These design elements, including slide layouts, themes, theme colors, and theme fonts, offer an inherent consistency that comes as a result of a common look and feel. This consistency means that you don't have to be a graphic designer to prepare an attractive presentation.

Layouts control how many and what types of placeholders appear on a slide. For example, a layout might contain only a slide title placeholder, or a slide title plus content placeholders. Themes can be applied to individual slides or to multiple slides in your presentation. A theme includes background colors, graphics, font styles and sizes, and alignment of placeholders and text. Theme colors are preset combinations of colors for your slide backgrounds, text, and graphic elements, whereas theme fonts are preset heading and body font combinations. You can further customize the look of a presentation by changing slide backgrounds and slide size.

In this section:

- Understanding what slide layouts and themes control
- Applying a layout
- Working with themes
- Changing theme colors and fonts
- Changing slide backgrounds and sizes

Understanding what slide layouts and themes control

Slide layouts provide a basic structure to your slides by including placeholders that can contain title or subtitle text, bulleted lists, or different kinds of graphic elements (referred to as content) in a variety of combinations. By selecting the right slide layout, you make the job of adding text and content easier because placeholders make building slides automatic.

Whereas slide layouts control the types of slide content, slide themes apply the design elements of a slide. These include a background color, fonts and colors used for various items in the presentation, and effects such as gradients. In addition, each of the built-in themes includes color variants that you can use to change the background color and the colors for other objects such as text.

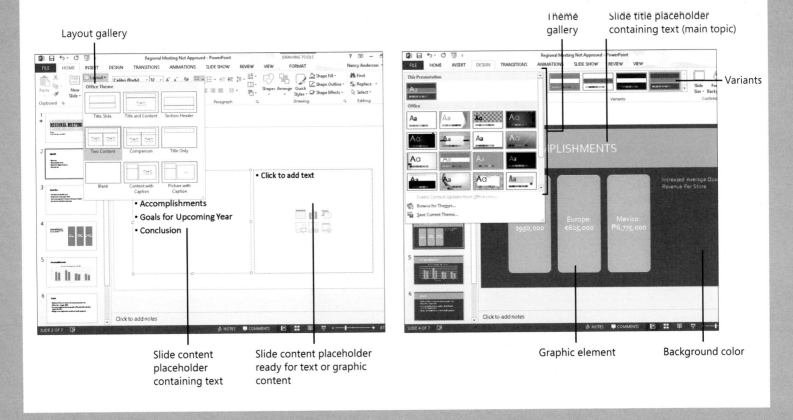

Layout gallery

Theme gallery

Slide title placeholder containing text (main topic)

Variants

Slide content placeholder containing text

Slide content placeholder ready for text or graphic content

Graphic element

Background color

Applying a layout

A slide layout in PowerPoint is like a blueprint for a house; it establishes the various types of "rooms" that appear on your slide. Just as certain types of rooms contain certain types of furniture, slides can contain different types of objects. A Title And Content slide holds a title and bullet list, whereas a Picture With Caption slide holds an image and some text that describes it. The placeholders in a layout automatically format the content you add, applying settings specific to each type of placeholder.

Apply a different layout to a slide

1 Display the slide whose layout you want to change and then, on the ribbon, click the Home tab.

2 In the Slides group, click Layout to open the Layout gallery.

3 Click a layout to apply it.

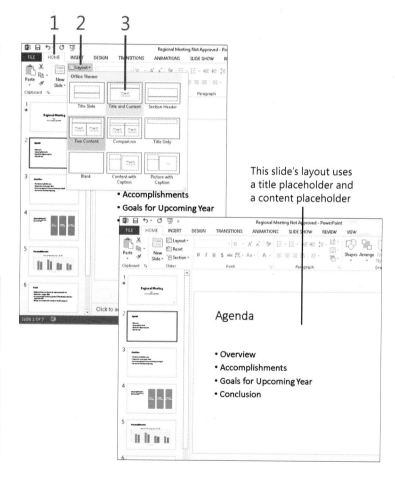

This slide's layout uses a title placeholder and a content placeholder

Working with themes

Themes in PowerPoint provide a suite of design settings and style definitions that give your slides a consistent look and feel. You can apply a theme in a single action, putting in place background graphics, colors, fonts, and effects. The gallery of themes located on the Design tab helps you preview and choose the best look for your presentation. You can further adjust the look of a presentation by choosing another color combination in the Variants group.

Change the theme

1 On the ribbon, click the Design tab.

2 In the Themes group, click the More arrow in the Themes gallery.

3 Move your mouse pointer over a theme to see a preview of it applied on your slides.

4 Right-click a theme. On the shortcut menu that opens, click one of two options:

- Choose Apply To All Slides to apply the theme to every slide in your presentation.

- Choose Apply To Selected Slides to apply the theme only to the currently selected slide or slides.

(continued on next page)

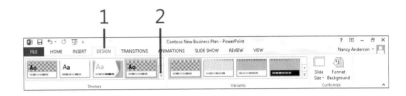

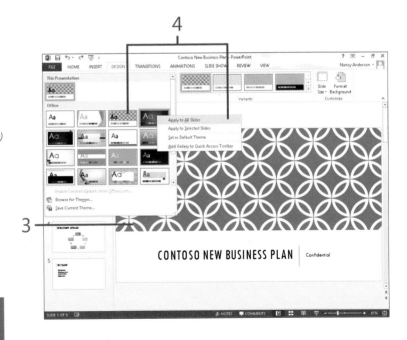

SEE ALSO For information about making individual changes to design elements on slides, see Section 11, "Formatting text and objects," starting on page 165.

Change the theme (continued)

5 In the Variants group, move your mouse pointer over a thumbnail to see a preview of its colors applied to the current slide.

6 Click the variant thumbnail to apply the colors to the slide.

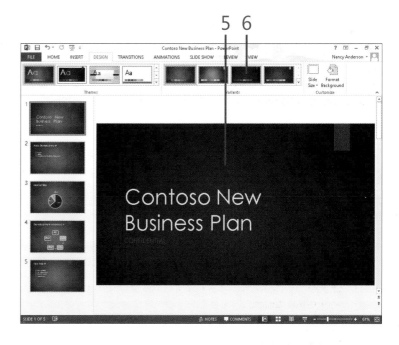

SEE ALSO When you apply a new theme, that process creates a master. For more information about working with slide masters, see "Understanding how slide masters work" on page 66.

TIP If you want to apply a theme to several slides, it's easiest to display Slide Sorter view, click the first slide to which you want to apply the theme, and then hold down the Ctrl key and click other slides. Follow the preceding task steps to apply the theme and variant to the selected slides.

Changing theme colors and fonts

Themes include settings for colors and fonts. A theme's color scheme affects most elements on your slide, including background, text, and graphics. Theme colors provide sets of colors that work well together, so the slides within your presentation maintain not only an attractive look, but a cohesive one, as well.

Theme fonts include settings for heading and body fonts. When you apply a theme, it contains a preset color scheme and fonts, but you can change the theme colors and theme fonts to give your slides a different look.

Select a different theme color scheme

1 On the ribbon, click the Design tab.

2 In the Variants group, click the More arrow in the Variants gallery.

3 On the menu that appears, point to Colors.

4 In the gallery that opens, click a color scheme to apply it to all slides. Or, you can right-click a color scheme and choose Apply To Selected Slides.

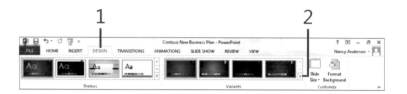

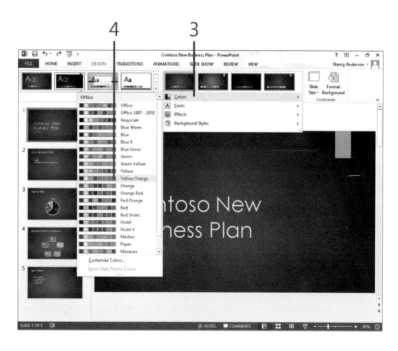

> **TIP** Be sure to use color combinations that work well in the space where you will give your presentation. Most color combinations PowerPoint offers should help to keep your text readable, but if you decide to change the color of an individual element yourself, remember that light text colors are hard to read in a lighted room.

> **TIP** After you click the More button in the Variants group, you can use the Effects choice to display the gallery of theme effects. From here you can apply another choice to the presentation.

Change theme fonts

1 On the ribbon, click the Design tab.

2 In the Variants group, click the More arrow in the Variants gallery.

3 On the menu that appears, point to Fonts.

4 In the gallery that opens, click a font style to apply it to all slides.

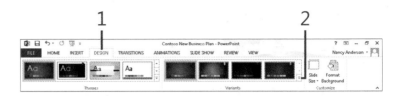

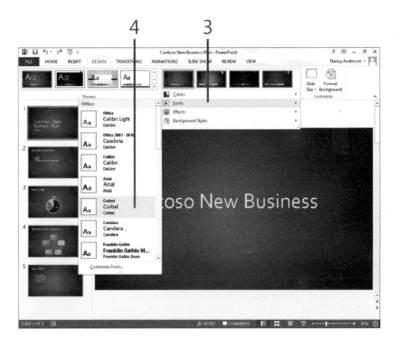

> **TRY THIS** To create your own theme font, in the theme fonts gallery, choose Customize Fonts. Select a heading font and body font, give the theme font a name, and then click Save. The theme is now available in the Fonts gallery.

> **TIP** After you change the theme colors and fonts, you can save your changes as a new, custom theme. In the Themes group, click the More button, click Save Current Theme, enter a name, and then click Save.

Changing slide backgrounds and sizes

In addition to theme settings, the slide background and size settings impact the overall appearance of a presentation. You can change the background for the current slide or for all slides in the presentation. You also can hide background graphics if they interfere with other graphics or content placeholders you've placed on a slide. Choose the slide size that best fits the monitor on which you intend to display your presentation.

Change the background color and hide graphics

1 On the ribbon, click the Design tab.

2 In the Customize group, click the Format Background button.

The Format Background pane opens.

3 Select the Hide Background Graphics check box.

4 Click Solid Fill.

5 Click the Fill Color button and then click a color in the palette.

6 To use the color on all slides, click Apply To All.

7 Click the pane Close (X) button.

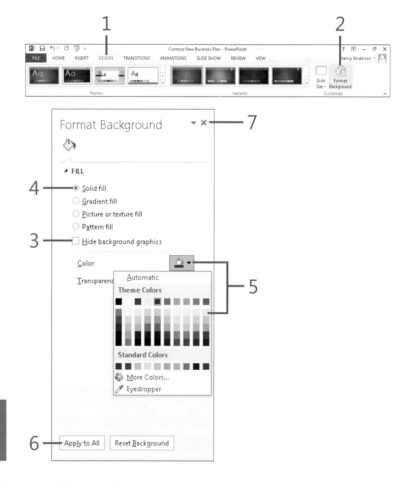

> **TIP** You can use the other choices in the Fill section in the Format Background pane to create gradient, picture, texture, or pattern fills.

Change the slide size

1 On the ribbon, click the Design tab.

2 In the Customize group, click the Slide Size button.

The available slide sizes appear.

3 Click the slide size to use for your presentation.

Use the Standard (4:3) size for older displays, projection, or TV equipment.

A dialog box opens, asking how to scale slide content based on the new slide size.

4 Click either Maximize or Ensure Fit.

The Maximize choice enlarges slide content to fill the slide size, and some content might be cut off; Ensure Fit reduces the size of slide content to fit on the new slide size.

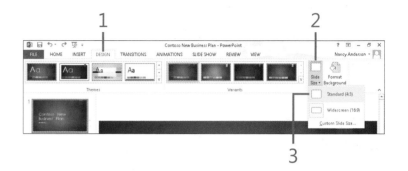

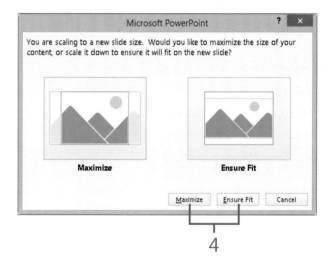

Inserting media and drawing objects

10

The ability to add graphical elements to your slides lets you add a visual pizzazz to your presentation that helps keep viewers entertained and interested. In a multimedia-savvy world, people expect more than black bullet points and a white background. Microsoft PowerPoint 2013 helps you meet those expectations.

Although visual elements should never overpower the message of your presentation, some visual elements such as photographs or charts might actually help you to convey difficult to describe concepts. Sometimes you use elements such as illustrations, shapes, or WordArt effects simply to add visual interest. By using video or audio clips, you can bring other people into the presentation to make a point, give a testimonial, or demonstrate a product feature.

In this section, you explore the process of inserting various visual elements into slides—tables, charts, pictures, WordArt, SmartArt, audio, and even video clips. After you insert such elements, move on to Section 11, "Formatting text and objects," starting on page 165, where you can see how to format and modify those elements to their best effect.

In this section:

- Working with tables
- Formatting tables
- Modifying tables
- Creating a chart
- Modifying a chart
- Inserting online pictures
- Inserting a picture from your SkyDrive
- Creating WordArt
- Working with SmartArt
- Working with local pictures
- Inserting local media objects
- Including online video
- Creating a photo album
- Drawing shapes and text boxes

Working with tables

You can use tables to arrange information in cells, organized by rows and columns, to show the relationships among various sets of data. Tables offer the option of formatting those columns and rows with color and shading, which helps the viewer to differentiate the sets of data at a glance.

Insert a table in a content placeholder

1 In Normal view, in the Thumbnails pane, click the slide that has the content placeholder in which you want to insert the table. Or, insert a new slide with a content placeholder via the Home tab.

2 In the content placeholder of the slide, click the Insert Table icon (upper left).

The Insert Table dialog box opens.

3 Specify the table size that you want by changing the entries in the Number Of Columns and Number Of Rows boxes.

4 Click OK to create an empty table.

(continued on next page)

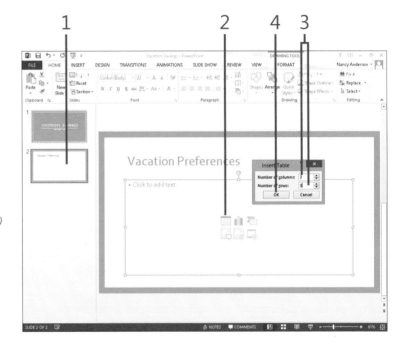

(continued on next page)

> **TRY THIS** You can also insert a table by using the Insert menu and choosing Table, and then clicking and dragging over the number of rows and columns you want in the grid that appears.

Insert a table in a content placeholder *(continued)*

The Table Tools Design and Table Tools Layout tabs appear when a table is selected.

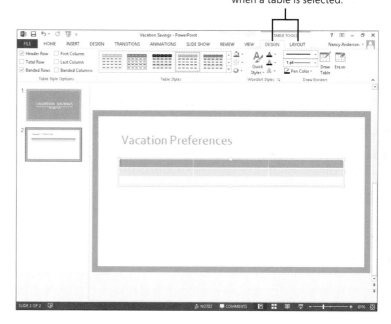

SEE ALSO This section deals with the basics of inserting tables. For more about formatting tables, see "Formatting tables" on page 131.

TRY THIS The Comparison slide layout includes a title placeholder, two subtitle placeholders, and two content placeholders. If you want to include two tables that viewers can compare side by side with a heading describing the contents of each, this is a useful layout to use.

Insert rows and columns

1 Click the table to select it.

2 Place your mouse pointer above a column or to the left of a row until the pointer turns into an arrow. Click to select the column or row.

3 On the ribbon, click the Table Tools|Layout contextual tab.

4 In the Rows & Columns group, click the Insert Left button or Insert Right button to insert a column to the left or right of the selected column, respectively.

5 In the Rows & Columns group, click the Insert Above button or Insert Below button to insert a row above or below the selected row, respectively.

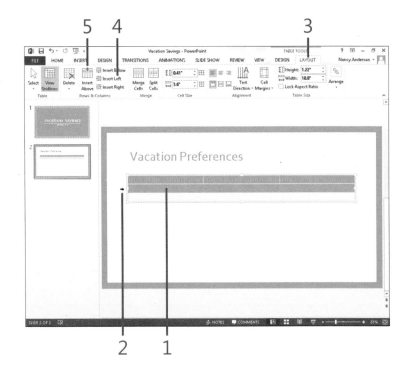

> **TIP** You can split the cells of a table column in two to include two sets of data without having to add a new column. Select the column as described in step 2 in this task. Next, on the Table Tools|Layout contextual tab, in the Merge group, click the Split Cells button. In the Split Cells dialog box that opens, adjust the Number Of Rows setting as needed and click OK. The column splits into two parts, and you can enter text in each.

Formatting tables

There are several things you can do to help make your tables easier to read. For example, you can add borders to cells to clearly separate the information. You can also align text in cells both horizontally and vertically. You can even merge two or more cells. For instance, you can merge cells so that the title of a table runs across all the columns in the table.

Modify table borders

1 Drag across a table to select all of its cells. Or, you could select individual cells to format, or a row or column.

2 On the ribbon, click the Table Tools|Design contextual tab.

3 In the Draw Borders group, click the drop-down arrow at the right side of the Border tool.

The Borders drop-down list appears.

(continued on next page)

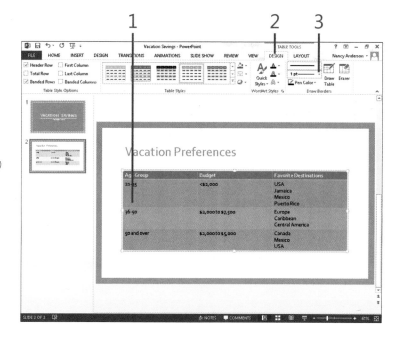

> **TRY THIS** Before applying borders, use the Pen Weight and Pen Color drop-down lists in the Draw Borders group of the Table Tools|Design contextual tab to choose the formatting to use for the new borders.

Modify table borders *(continued)*

4 Choose a border style such as All Borders to outline each and every cell in the table, or Outside Borders to surround the outside of the selected cells with a border.

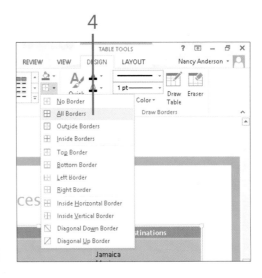

🔍 **SEE ALSO** For information about formatting table styles and adding background colors, see "Formatting an object fill" on page 171.

Align text in cells

1 Drag across the cells to select those whose text you want to align.

2 On the ribbon, click the Table Tools|Layout contextual tab.

(continued on next page)

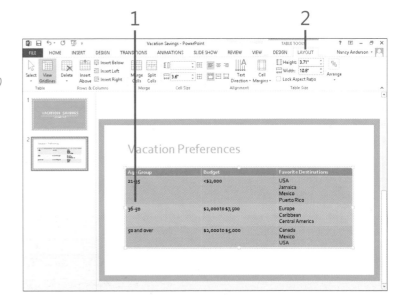

Align text in cells *(continued)*

3 In the Alignment group, click the Align Left, Center, or Align Right buttons, as desired, to align the text relative to the sides of the cell.

4 In the Alignment group, click the Align Top, Center Vertically, or Align Bottom buttons to align the text between the top and bottom of the cells.

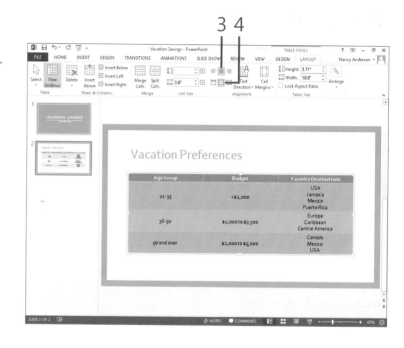

TIP You can also click the Arrange button on the Home tab, click Align Text, and then click any of the alignment commands on the menu that appears.

TRY THIS To align a table relative to the edges of your slides, at the right end of the Table Tools|Layout contextual tab, click Arrange, point to Align, and then choose Align To Slide. (At a high screen resolution, you might not need to click Arrange first.)

Modifying tables

In addition to changing the appearance of a table, you can adjust it by working with its cells. You might want to merge two or more selected cells together to form one larger cell. For example, you might want to do this to create a title cell that applies to multiple columns of information below it. You also can delete unneeded rows or columns from a table, or delete the entire table.

Merge cells

1   Drag to select the cells that you want to merge.

2   On the ribbon, click the Table Tools|Layout contextual tab.

3   In the Merge group, click Merge Cells.

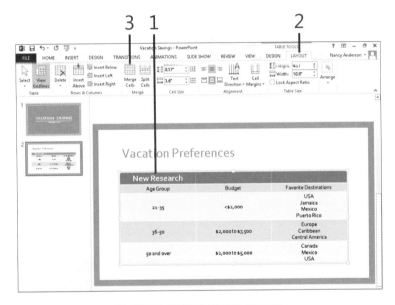

> **TRY THIS**   To return the merged cell to individual cells again, drag to select the merged cell. Then, on the Table Tools|Layout contextual tab, in the Merge group, click the Split Cells button. In the dialog box that appears, enter the number of columns or rows into which you want to split the merged cell and then click OK.

> **TIP**   You can merge any number of cells, including cells in multiple rows and columns. This is often useful for tables that you use to create forms, which might have nonuniform cells for holding different types of information or pictures of various sizes.

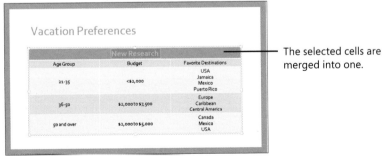

The selected cells are merged into one.

Delete rows, columns, or the table

1 Select the table. To delete a particular row or column, place your mouse pointer above a column or to the left of a row until the pointer turns into an arrow and then click to select the column or row.

2 On the ribbon, click the Table Tools|Layout contextual tab.

3 In the Rows & Columns group, click the Delete button.

4 On the menu that opens, click Delete Columns or Delete Rows (depending on whether you selected a column or row in step 1), or click Delete Table.

> **TIP** After you delete a table, the tools for adding content to the content placeholder reappear. You then have the option of adding other content, including a new table. This might be the fastest method when you realize you're not satisfied with a table's layout and adding and removing rows and columns would be too time-consuming.

Creating a chart

Charts in PowerPoint 2013 are based on the charting feature in Microsoft Excel. When you insert a chart, Excel opens so that you can enter the underlying data. When Excel opens, it displays some sample data, which should help you enter your specific data in the proper format to form the basis of a chart. Charts are wonderful tools for providing lots of information in a quickly understood, visual format. The chart feature in PowerPoint offers dozens of styles of charts.

Insert a chart

1 In Normal view, in the Thumbnails pane, click the slide that has the content placeholder in which you want to insert the chart. Or, insert a new slide with a content placeholder via the Home tab.

2 In the content placeholder of the slide, click the Insert Chart icon (top center).

The Insert Chart dialog box opens.

(continued on next page)

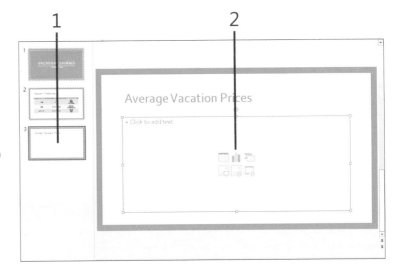

TIP Many of the chart types are suitable for illustrating trends over time or for comparing data. The last several chart categories—XY (Scatter), Stock, Surface, Radar, and Combo—are for special purpose situations. Take the time to research the various chart types by using the Help feature to ensure that you choose one that's suitable for your data. Also, take a close look at the thumbnail that appears when you select a chart style. This will help you to get a sense of what your chart might look like.

Insert a chart *(continued)*

3 On the left, click a category of chart type that you want to insert.

4 Along the top, click a chart style.

5 Click OK.

(continued on next page)

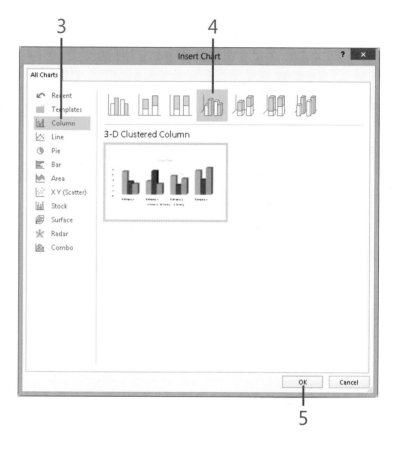

TIP You can change the chart type at any time by clicking Change Chart Type in the Type group on the Chart Tools|Design contextual tab. The Change Chart Type dialog box (which is identical to the Create Chart dialog box) opens, allowing you to select another type of chart.

Insert a chart *(continued)*

6 Modify the sample data with your own source data for the chart.

7 Click the Close button in the Excel window to return to PowerPoint and view the chart.

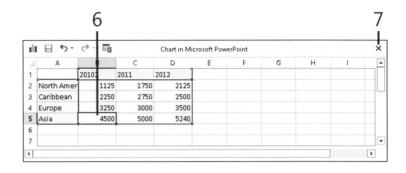

The chart appears on your PowerPoint slide.

Modifying a chart

Using the Chart Tools|Design contextual tab in PowerPoint 2013, you can make fast overall changes to chart design. Change the layout for the chart to determine what items (title, legend, and so on) appear on the chart. Choose another chart style to adjust the chart fills, effects, and other formatting. You can further modify the layout that you've applied by showing or hiding the legend, which identifies the series in the chart.

Change chart style and layout

1 Click a chart to select it.

2 On the ribbon, click the Chart Tools|Design contextual tab.

3 In the Chart Layouts group, click Quick Layout.

   The Quick Layout gallery opens.

4 Click a new layout to apply it.

5 On the Chart Styles gallery, click the More button to show available chart styles.

(continued on next page)

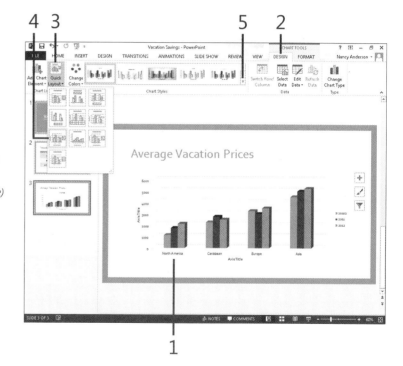

Change chart style and layout *(continued)*

6 Click a new style to apply it.

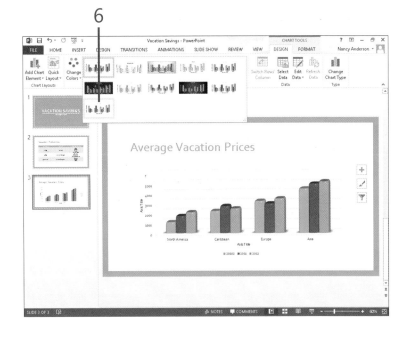

TIP A layout applies formatting to your chart, but you can modify each aspect of the chart layout manually by using the tools on the Chart Tools|Design contextual tab. The next task explains how to modify the legend display, for example.

Display or hide the chart legend

1 Click a chart to select it.

2 On the ribbon, click the Chart Tools|Design contextual tab.

3 In the Chart Layouts group, click the Add Chart Element button.

The Add Chart Element drop-down list appears.

4 Point to Legend.

5 Click a layout position for the legend or click None to turn the legend off.

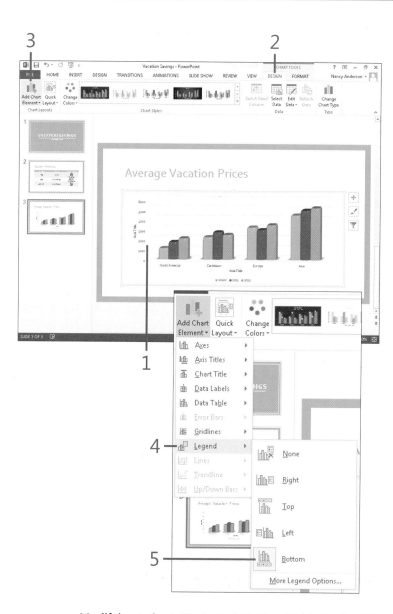

TIP Instead of choosing a placement for the legend by selecting a layout or by using the Legend button, you can move the legend to any position you want by dragging it within the chart area.

TRY THIS You can format a legend by right-clicking it in the chart and then, on the shortcut menu that appears, clicking Format Legend. In the Format Legend pane that appears, you can modify the position of the legend and the line style surrounding it, add a fill color as a background for it, and so on.

Including online pictures in your presentation

A chart content placeholder gives you the option of inserting pictures into your PowerPoint 2013 presentation from online sources. You can search for royalty-free pictures through the Office.com Clip Art collection.

Insert online pictures

1 In Normal view, in the Thumbnails pane, click the slide that has the content placeholder in which you want to insert the online picture. Or, insert a new slide with a content placeholder via the Home tab.

2 In the content placeholder of the slide, click the Online Pictures icon (bottom center).

The Insert Pictures dialog box opens.

3 Type a search term in the Office.com Clip Art search box.

4 Click the Search button or press Enter.

The Office.com Clip Art window shows pictures and illustrations matching the search term. Scroll down the list to see the results.

(continued on next page)

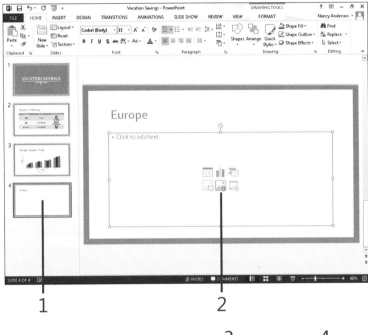

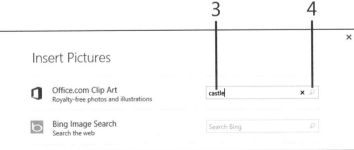

TRY THIS The Picture Tools|Format contextual tab appears any time you select an inserted picture. Explore the tools available on this tab. You can learn more about these in Section 11, "Formatting text and objects," starting on page 165.

Insert online pictures *(continued)*

5 Click the picture to insert. Or, double-click the picture and skip to step 7.

6 Click Insert.

7 Click the slide background to deselect the picture.

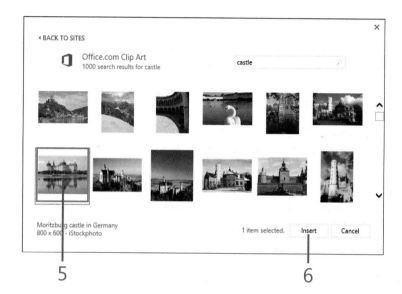

5   6

7

TIP The process for searching for images via Bing is similar to the process for Office.com. Just use the Bing Image Search box in step 3. Images on Bing are offered under the Creative Commons licensing scheme, which means images will use different types of permissions. For example, some will restrict image usage to non-commercial purposes or require attribution. Be sure that you carefully check the licensing terms for any image you select from a Bing search.

Inserting a picture from your SkyDrive

You can download pictures from your SkyDrive or an online photo service such as Flickr. By taking advantage of this expanded new resource, you can make your PowerPoint 2013 slides come alive visually.

Insert a picture from your SkyDrive

1 In Normal view, in the Thumbnails pane, click the slide that has the content placeholder in which you want to insert the picture. Or, insert a new slide with a content placeholder via the Home tab.

2 In the content placeholder of the slide, click the Online Pictures icon (bottom center).

   The Insert Pictures dialog box opens.

3 Click the Browse link to the right of your SkyDrive.

   The SkyDrive window shows folders on the SkyDrive.

(continued on next page)

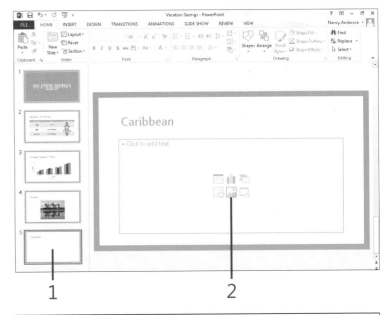

TIP The picture you insert from your SkyDrive must be in one of the formats supported by PowerPoint, which include TIFF, JPEG, PNG, GIF, or BMP.

Insert a picture from your SkyDrive *(continued)*

4 Click the folder that contains the picture you want to insert.

5 Click the picture to insert. Or, double-click the picture and skip Step 6.

6 Click Insert.

The picture appears on the slide. Click outside it to deselect it.

4

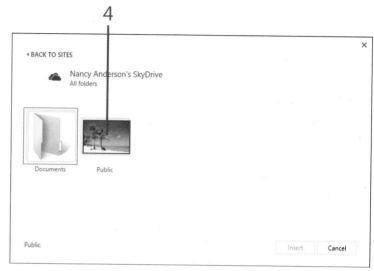

5

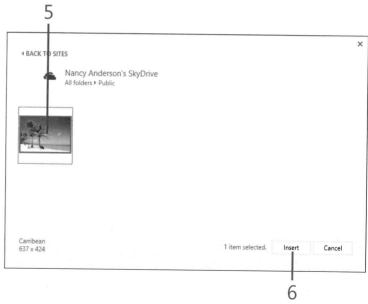

6

TIP You can share images in a folder on your SkyDrive with other users. For example, if you're on a team developing a new product brochure and other new product documentation, you can put all the product images in a public or shared SkyDrive folder so that team members can access them while working on the various documents.

Creating visual text effects by using WordArt

WordArt is a tool you can use to apply interesting effects such as curves or 3-D views to any PowerPoint 2013 text. WordArt is best used to call attention to short phrases, such as "Free!" or "All New" because the distortions of WordArt designs can make longer phrases hard to read. You first insert a WordArt placeholder, enter text into the placeholder, and then apply various effects.

Insert WordArt

1. With the slide in which you want to insert the WordArt selected, click the Insert tab.

2. In the Text group, click WordArt.

3. In the gallery that opens, click a WordArt style.

4. Type your text in the placeholder.

5. Click outside the placeholder to view the WordArt.

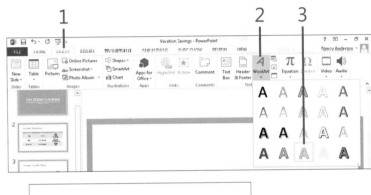

TRY THIS You can also select text in your presentation and then follow the steps to insert WordArt. In this case, the WordArt placeholder appears with the selected text already displayed in it.

TIP You can resize WordArt easily by clicking it to select it and then dragging one of the selection handles out or in. To keep the object's original proportions, be sure to drag only a corner handle.

Apply effects to WordArt

1 Click the WordArt object to select it.

2 On the ribbon, click the Drawing Tools|Format contextual tab.

3 In the WordArt Styles group, click the Text Effects button.

The WordArt Text Effects categories drop-down list appears.

(continued on next page)

Apply effects to WordArt *(continued)*

4 Move your mouse pointer over a category to display the styles gallery for that category.

5 Move your pointer over various effects to preview them on your WordArt object.

6 Click an effect to apply it to the WordArt. You can apply multiple categories of effects.

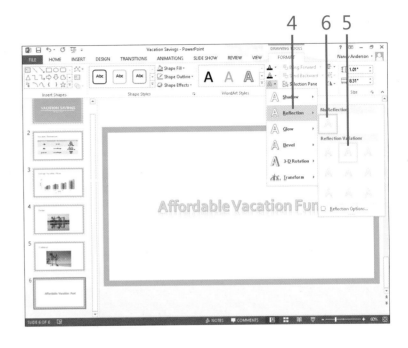

> **✓ TIP** If the effect only previews on one word in the WordArt in step 4, it means you don't have the full WordArt object selected. If that happens, click a blank area to close the Text Effects menu. Click the dashed border around the WordArt object to change it to a solid border. Then, apply the desired effect.

Working with SmartArt

PowerPoint 2013 offers SmartArt, an enhanced diagramming tool that you can use to quickly create all kinds of diagrams and workflow charts. After you select and insert a SmartArt diagram, you can then use a simple outline pane to enter the text that populates the various boxes and shapes in the diagram. You can insert or delete elements easily. SmartArt also works like the shapes built into PowerPoint, so after you insert a diagram, you can change various characteristics of it by altering its shapes, adding shapes, modifying their colors, and more.

Insert SmartArt

1 In Normal view, in the Thumbnails pane, click the slide that has the content placeholder in which you want to insert the SmartArt object. Or, insert a new slide with a content placeholder via the Home tab.

2 In the content placeholder of the slide, click the Insert A SmartArt Graphic icon (upper right).

The Choose A SmartArt Graphic dialog box opens.

(continued on next page)

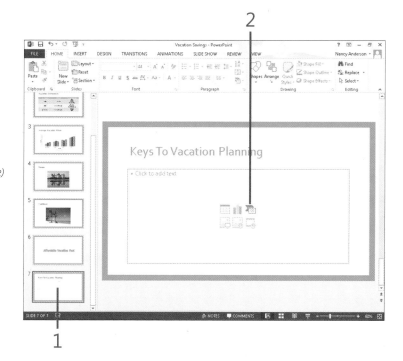

Insert SmartArt *(continued)*

3 Click a category on the left.

4 Click a style in the center pane to see a preview of it on the right.

5 Click OK to insert the SmartArt object.

> ⊙ **SEE ALSO** For more information about working with objects on your slides, see Section 11, "Formatting text and objects," on page 165.

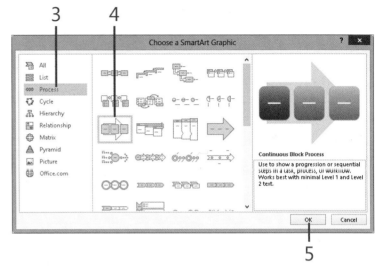

Add text to SmartArt

1 Click a SmartArt object to open it for editing.

2 If needed, click the left-arrow button at center left of the object to open the Text pane.

3 Click in a shape object labelled [Text] in the SmartArt and type the text for the first shape.

(continued on next page)

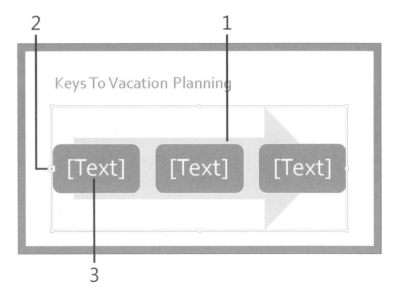

Add text to SmartArt (continued)

4 Click in the next [Text] placeholder in the pane and type the text. It appears in the next bullet or shape.

The text appears in the text pane to the left of the SmartArt; you can also enter your text here. Continue until you've finished adding the text. Text appears in the SmartArt graphic shapes. If you want to add an additional heading, press Enter after typing a top-level entry.

5 When you've finished adding the text, click outside the shape.

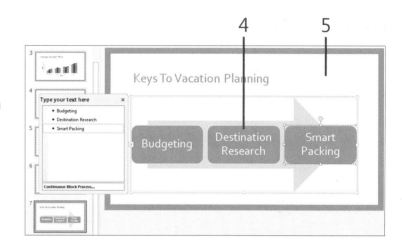

TIP The Tab key works differently in the SmartArt Text pane. If you press Tab after clicking a [TEXT] placeholder, the insertion point does not move to the next line as it does in some forms and programs. Instead, pressing Tab indents the line one level. If you click a [TEXT] placeholder and press Shift+Tab, the line moves up one level in the outline.

TIP Some SmartArt styles include picture icons. Click these to display the Insert Picture window. You use this in the same way as you do for the tasks described in other parts in this section for locating and inserting a picture file. This feature is useful for diagrams such as organizational charts in which you want to insert photos of individuals in the organization.

Working with local pictures

If you have your own photos available, you can use them in PowerPoint 2013 to add impact to your presentation. Perhaps you have a photo of your newest product for a sales presentation. Or, maybe you want to include a photo of your soccer team in action for a school sports presentation. Placing a photo onto a slide is easy to do. After a picture is inserted, you can trim away any unwanted portions by using the Crop tool.

Insert a picture from a file

1 In Normal view, in the Thumbnails pane, click the slide that has the content placeholder in which you want to insert the image. Or, insert a new slide with a content placeholder via the Home tab.

2 In the content placeholder of the slide, click the Pictures icon (lower left).

    The Insert Picture dialog box opens.

(continued on next page)

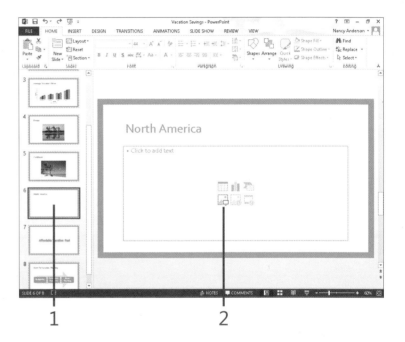

SEE ALSO   The Photo Album feature makes it possible for you to create groups of photos to help organize your images. For more about this feature, see "Creating a photo album" on page 159.

Insert a picture from a file *(continued)*

3 Locate the picture file that you want to insert and click to select it.

4 Click Insert.

The picture appears on the slide.

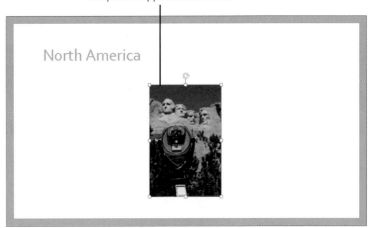

TIP You can insert a picture anywhere on a slide by clicking the Pictures button in the Images group on the Insert tab.

Crop a picture

1 Click a picture to select it.

2 On the ribbon, click the Picture Tools|Format contextual tab.

3 In the Size group, click Crop.

4 Drag any of the heavy cropping handles that appear around the edge of the picture inward to crop the picture. Continue cropping from various sides until the picture appears as you want.

5 Press the Esc key, or click anywhere outside the picture to turn off the Crop tool.

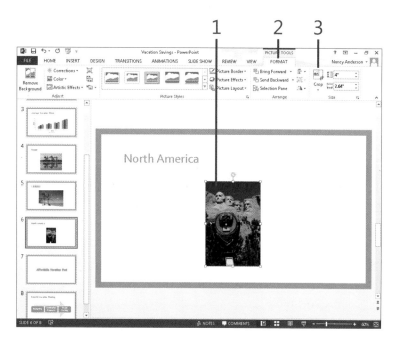

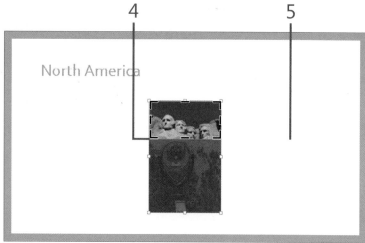

> **TIP** If you just want a smaller picture, you can resize it rather than cropping some of the picture away. To resize a picture, select it, click any of the handles that appear, and then drag in or out. To maintain the picture's proportions, use the any of the corner handles to adjust the size.

> **TIP** If you crop too much from your picture, you can use the Crop tool to drag outward to restore the portion you cropped. You can do this even after deactivating the cropping session in which you first trimmed the picture.

Inserting local media objects

Sprinkling sounds and video into your PowerPoint 2013 presentations can add some sparkle or even help to bring a point home with flair. Multimedia objects in your slides are represented by an icon, depending on which type of object it is; a video object is indicated by an illustration icon, and an audio object is indicated by a small speaker icon. You can choose to play the video or sound object as soon as the slide it's placed on appears or when you click the object while running in Slide Show view.

Insert video or audio from a file

1 With the slide in which you want to insert the audio or video selected, click the Insert tab.

2 In the Media group, click the Video button or Audio button.

3 On the menu that appears, click Video On My PC or Audio On My PC.

   The Insert Audio or Insert Video dialog box opens, depending on which you're inserting.

4 Locate and select the file that you want to insert and click Insert.

(continued on next page)

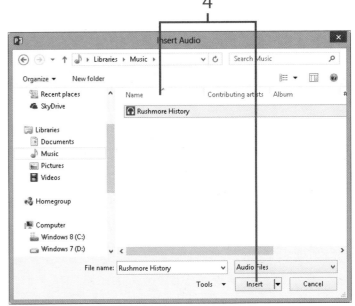

Insert video or audio from a file *(continued)*

5 Click the Play/Pause button in the toolbar beneath the media icon to preview the file.

6 Depending on what you inserted, click either the Video Tools|Playback or the Audio Tools|Playback contextual tab, click the arrow on the Start field, and then click Automatically or On Click to select how you want the object to run.

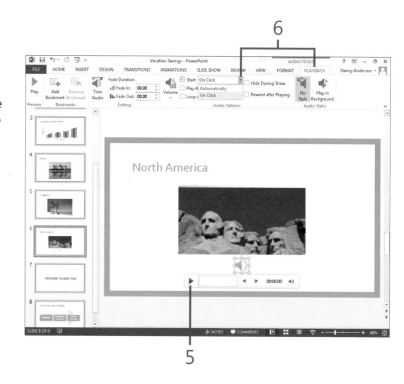

> **TIP** If you set up a media clip to play automatically when a slide appears during a slide show, it plays once. If you want to play it again, click the object.

Including online video

You can insert online video from Bing Video Search and other sources directly into a PowerPoint 2013 content placeholder.

Insert online video

1 On a slide with a content placeholder, click the Insert Video icon (lower right) in the content placeholder.

The Insert Video dialog box opens.

(continued on next page)

Insert online video *(continued)*

2 In the Bing Video Search box, type a search term.

3 Click the Search button or press Enter.

The Bing Video Search window shows videos matching the search term. Scroll down the list to see the results.

4 Click the video that you want to insert.

5 Click Insert.

On the Video Tools|Format contextual tab, in the Preview group, click the Play button to view the video.

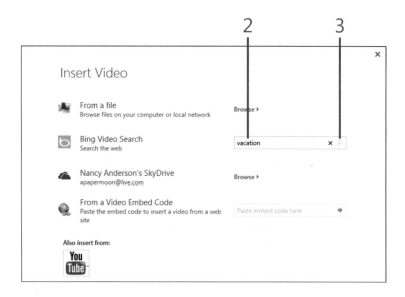

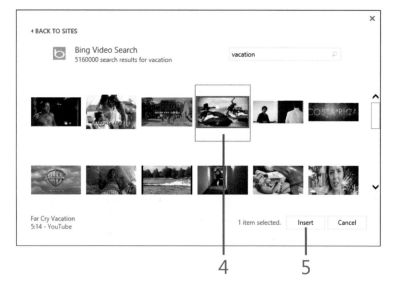

> **TIP** Content placeholders don't offer an icon for inserting online audio. You can insert online audio on any slide as described in "Insert online audio" on page 25.

Creating a photo album

If you want to create a new slide show that consists of a series of photos, you can use a feature in Microsoft PowerPoint 2013 called Photo Album. A photo album is a tool that you can use to set up a series of photos and text boxes, one each per slide in sequence. You can include captions for the photos, and you can also make use of photo editing tools included in the Photo Album feature. Using these tools, you can rotate photos or change their brightness or contrast.

Insert a new photo album

1 On the ribbon, click the Insert tab.

2 In the Images group, click Photo Album. (Click the button itself, not the drop-down arrow.)

The Photo Album dialog box opens.

3 Click the File/Disk button.

The Insert New Pictures dialog box opens.

4 Locate a picture to insert and click the Insert button. Repeat this for as many photos as you want to include in the album.

(continued on next page)

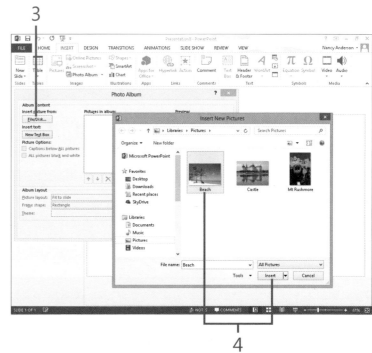

Insert a new photo album *(continued)*

5 If you want to include a text slide, click the New Text Box button.

6 Use any of the tools to modify your photo album.

7 Click Create to save the album.

The new album is created. Save it as a stand-alone presentation or insert it into a larger presentation.

Click to select picture options such as using captions or showing all photos in black and white.

Use these settings to change the layout of the photos; for example, to include two pictures per slide or to change the shape of the photos to oval or beveled.

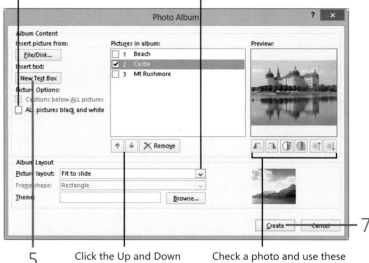

5

Click the Up and Down arrow buttons to change the sequence of photos.

Check a photo and use these tools to rotate the image or adjust the brightness or contrast.

→ **TRY THIS** You can edit a photo album after you've created it. Click the drop-down arrow on the Photo Album button and then click Edit Photo Album. In the Edit Photo Album dialog box, use the tools to remove photos, add photos, rearrange photos, or change any of the picture or layout options.

🔍 **SEE ALSO** After you create a photo album, you can modify the individual pictures by resizing, rotating, or moving them on the slides. For more information about working with objects, see "Rotating and flipping objects" on page 178.

Drawing shapes and text boxes

You can use the Shapes feature in PowerPoint 2013 to draw a variety of objects—from lines, arrows, and boxes, to scrolls, callouts, and action buttons. When you draw a shape, you can enter text in it; however, that text does not appear in your presentation outline. If you draw an action button, you can then associate an action with that button, such as running another

program or playing a sound when you click the button during a slide show. In addition to various shapes, you can draw a text box, which is simply a placeholder in which you can enter text. By default, a text box has no border, so the text appears to float on your page. Keep in mind that just like text in shapes, text in text boxes is not reflected in the presentation outline.

Draw a shape

1 With the slide in which you want to insert the shape selected, click the Insert tab.

2 In the Illustrations group, click Shapes.

The Shapes gallery opens below the button.

3 Click a shape. Your mouse pointer turns into a plus sign.

(continued on next page)

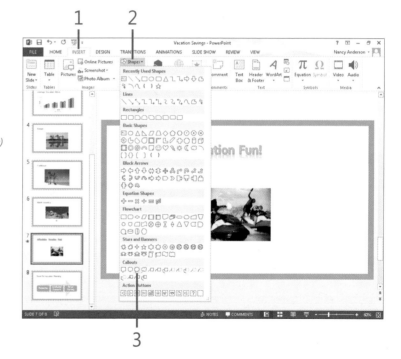

Draw a shape *(continued)*

4 Drag to draw the shape to whatever size you need. Or, simply click the slide to insert the shape at the default size.

5 If you want to add text to the shape, just type it.

6 If you add an action button, the Action Settings dialog box opens, in which you can choose to hyperlink to another slide, a presentation, or a website URL (use the drop-down list to select the target of the link); run a program; run a macro; initiate an action; or play a sound. Configure the settings that you need.

7 Click OK to save the settings.

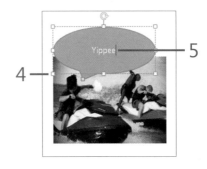

✓ TIP There are two tabs in the Action Settings dialog box: Mouse Click and Mouse Over. Depending on which tab you use to make settings, the action is initiated when you click the object or when you pass your mouse pointer over the object during the presentation.

Add a text box

1 With the slide in which you want to insert the text box selected, click the Insert tab.

2 In the Text group, click Text Box.

The mouse pointer turns into a plus sign.

3 Drag on the slide to draw the text box, which remains open for editing.

4 Type text and then click outside the box.

> **TIP** You can format a text box. To do so, right-click the text and then, on the shortcut menu that appears, click Format Shape. In the Format Shape pane, use the various categories of settings to add fill color, an outside border, 3-D and rotation effects, and more. When you select a shape you've drawn, the Drawing Tools|Format contextual tab becomes available, which you can also use to make formatting changes.

> **SEE ALSO** In addition to adding action buttons to your slides, you can use effects such as animations and transitions to make your presentation more dynamic. See Section 12, "Adding transitions and animations," starting on page 193, for more about working with these actions.

Formatting text and objects

11

When you apply a theme to your presentation, you're setting font styles and colors, but sometimes you might want to modify those styles or format some of the text for emphasis.

In addition to formatting text, placing a picture, a piece of line art, or a shape on a slide helps to add some interest to your presentation, but it's important that you make the object fit your overall design. That might mean resizing or rotating the object to align it better with other elements on the slide, or you might need to modify the color or brightness of an image to match your slide color scheme.

You can group objects that you insert on your slide so that you can move or modify them as one object. You can also set the *layering* order for objects so that one appears on top of another if they overlap. Microsoft PowerPoint 2013 includes a new Merge Shapes feature with which you can combine multiple overlapped objects in a variety of ways. Finally, Power-Point provides tools that you can use to customize pictures and videos in your presentation.

In this section:

- Applying text basics
- Formatting text
- Formatting an object fill
- Working with shape outlines and effects
- Resizing and deleting objects
- Rotating and flipping objects
- Grouping and ungrouping objects
- Changing the order of and merging objects
- Working with picture tools
- Using video tools

Applying text basics

Fonts are sets of design styles that you can apply to your text. They add a distinct personality to your slide contents. Some fonts are playful, whereas others are more formal. And then there are fonts that are great for adding emphasis. The trick to choosing the right font for a presentation is to ensure that it fits the design mood and purpose of your slides. You should also be sure that your audience can read it without difficulty, in whatever setting you show your presentation. To help ensure that, you can also change the font size if you need to.

Select a font

1 On the ribbon, click the Home tab.

2 Select the text that you want to format.

   You can either click the placeholder and then click its border to select all the text within it (the border becomes solid) or click the placeholder and then drag over a text selection within the placeholder.

3 In the Font group, click the drop-down arrow on the Font list.

4 Move your mouse pointer down the list of fonts, scrolling down as needed.

   Each font is previewed on the selected text as you move the pointer through the list.

5 Click the font that you want to apply to the selected text.

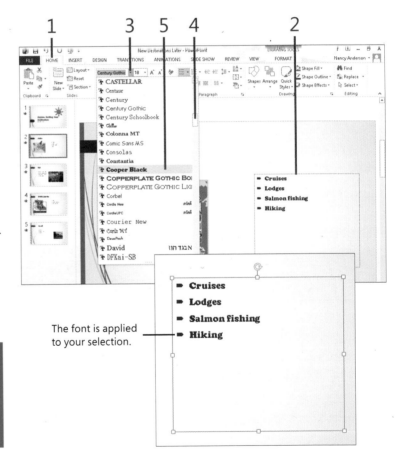

The font is applied to your selection.

> ✓ **TIP** The fonts you see on the Font list are those that are installed as a part of the Windows operating system. You can find additional font sets online, some free and some that you pay for. To learn more about fonts and to find additional font sets, visit the Microsoft Typography website at *www.microsoft.com/typography/default.mspx*.

Change text size

1 On the ribbon, click the Home tab.

2 Select the text that you want to resize.

You can either click the placeholder and then click its border to select all the text within it (the border becomes solid) or click the placeholder and then drag over a text selection within the placeholder.

3 In the Font group, click the Font Size drop-down arrow.

4 Move your pointer over the sizes to preview them on the selected text.

5 Click a size to apply it to the selected text.

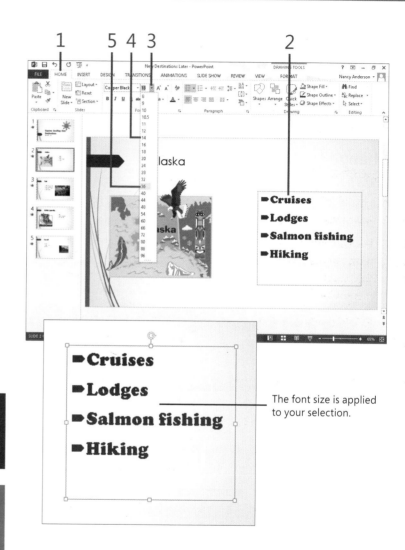

The font size is applied to your selection.

TRY THIS Not every single font size is available on the Font Size list. Only very commonly used sizes are included. If you find you need a size in between the preset ones, you can also type a size, such as 100, 13, or 30, in the Font Size box and press Enter to apply it.

TIP Don't make your text so small that it is difficult to read. Also, notice that as you add text to a placeholder, font sizes might shrink to accommodate all the text. By keeping font sizes large enough to read and your placeholder text to no more than six or so short bullet points, you ensure that your viewers can see your presentation content clearly.

Formatting text

There are several things you can do in PowerPoint 2013 to help make your text more interesting or more easily readable, including resizing it, changing its color, or applying effects such as bold, italic, or underline. Design themes apply preset font sizes and colors, but when you want to fit more text on a page or emphasize some text, the ability to resize text is handy. When you want to call attention to certain text, changing its color or making it bold, for example, can make it stand out.

Change text color

1 On the ribbon, click the Home tab.

2 Select the text that you want to format. Either select the entire placeholder or some of the text within the placeholder.

3 In the Font group, click the Font Color drop-down arrow.

4 In the Font Color gallery that opens, move your mouse pointer over the colors to preview them on the selected text.

(continued on next page)

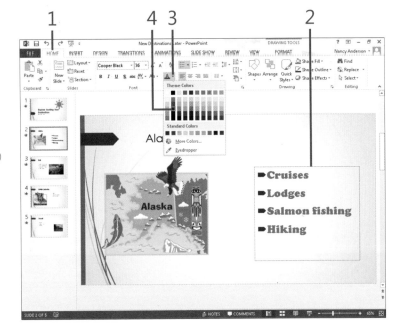

> **TIP** Be careful about choosing light colors that are hard to read (unless your slides have a dark background against which a light color can stand out). Likewise, don't choose dark font colors to use against a dark background. Remember, one of the most important aspects of your presentation is that viewers can easily read it!

Change text color *(continued)*

5 At the bottom of the Font Color gallery, click the More Colors option to view additional choices.

The Colors dialog box opens.

6 Click either the Standard tab or the Custom tab.

7 Click a color choice.

The Custom tab presents controls for the red-green-blue (RGB) color system. On this tab, you have many more color choices, and you can specify precise values for each of the three color settings.

8 Click OK to close the Color dialog box and apply the new color.

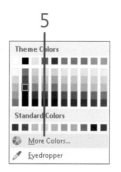

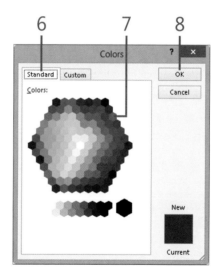

 TIP You can also use the mini toolbar that appears when you select text to change the font size and color or apply effects.

SEE ALSO To change the background color of your slides so that it works with your font color choices, see "Change the background color and hide graphics" on page 124.

Apply attributes to text

1 On the ribbon, click the Home tab.

2 Select the text that you want to format. Either select the entire placeholder or some of the text within the placeholder.

3 In the Font group, click any of the following buttons to apply that format to the selected text:

- Bold
- Italic
- Underline
- Strikethrough
- Shadow

4 Click the drop-down arrow on the Character Spacing button.

5 Click the spacing that you prefer. This ranges from Very Tight to Very Loose.

Very tight spacing pushes letters close together; very loose spacing places them farther apart.

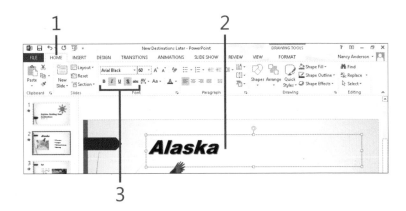

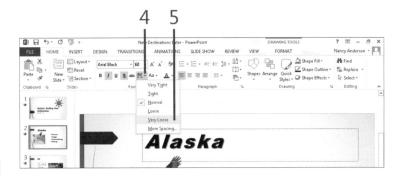

> **⊕ TRY THIS** To create custom character spacing, click the More Spacing option on the Character Spacing list. In the Font dialog box that appears, in the Character Spacing tab, choose Expanded or Condensed from the Spacing list and then specify by how many points this effect should be applied. Click OK to save the new setting.

> **✓ TIP** The character spacing between certain pairs of letters, such as AW, is also known as *kerning*. On the Character Spacing tab in the Font dialog box, you can specify that the kerning you apply be used only for fonts of a certain size or larger by selecting the Kerning For Fonts check box and selecting a font size.

Formatting an object fill

Objects, including clip art, WordArt, pictures, and shapes that you draw on your PowerPoint 2013 slides, can all be formatted in several ways. For example, you can fill an object with a color or a pattern.

Apply a fill color, gradient, or texture

1 Select a shape, text box, or WordArt object. (You can also perform these steps with SmartArt objects, but the Format tab in the next step is then named SmartArt Tools.)

2 Click the Drawing Tools|Format contextual tab.

3 In the Shape Styles group, click the Shape Fill button.

The Shape Fill gallery opens.

(continued on next page)

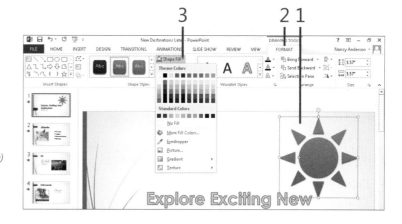

TRY THIS The Shape Fill gallery uses the Live Preview feature. When you pass your mouse pointer over a Theme Color or Standard Color or over a Gradient or Texture option, it is previewed on the selected object on your slide.

Apply a fill color, gradient, or texture (continued)

4 Click a Theme or Standard color to apply it.

Explore other settings.

Click More Fill Colors to display a dialog box offering custom color options.

Click No Fill to clear the inside of the object.

Click Picture to open a dialog box you can use to locate a picture to insert in the object.

Click Gradient or Texture to display a submenu of choices.

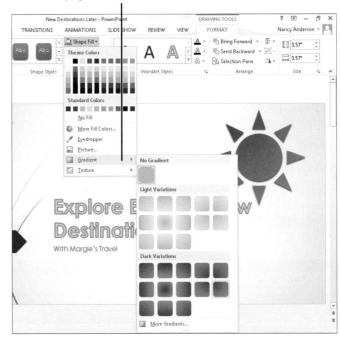

TIP You cannot add a fill to clip art or a picture object because their "fill" is the image they contain. However, you can change their shape or border or add effects such as 3-D. See the various related tasks elsewhere in this section to learn how.

Working with shape outlines and effects

In addition to filling an object with a color or a pattern, in PowerPoint 2013, you can change the outline of the shape by modifying the line style and thickness. You can also apply a wide variety of effects such as softening the edges or applying a three-dimensional (3-D) or rotation effect. Together, these formatting options make it possible for you to customize an object to appear just the way you want it.

Change the shape outline

1 In the Slides pane, click an object in a slide to select it.

2 On the ribbon, click either the Drawing Tools|Format or the Picture Tools|Format contextual tab (depending on whether you've selected a picture or another type of object).

3 In the Pictures Styles group, click the Picture Border button. (Or, in the Shape Styles group, click the Shape Outline button, again, depending on what you've selected in the slide.)

The Picture Border gallery opens.

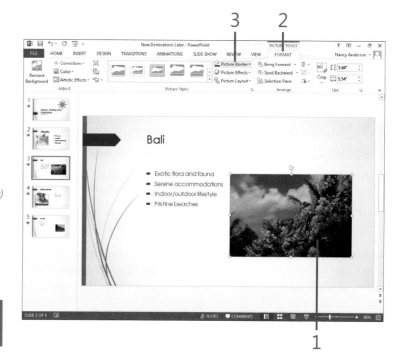

(continued on next page)

(continued on next page)

> **SEE ALSO** If you want to format a placeholder rather than an object, see "Format placeholders" on page 96.

> **TIP** Most PowerPoint color galleries now include the Eyedropper choice, which you can use to copy a color from a picture or other object on the slide. Click Eyedropper in the gallery, and then click the color in the object on the slide to select it and apply that color to other objects.

Change the shape outline *(continued)*

4 Use the gallery to make the changes that you want to the selected object.

- To display a dialog box offering custom color options, click More Outline Colors.

- To display a submenu of formatting choices for the picture border or shape outline, click Weight, Dashes, or Arrows (drawing objects only).

- To clear any outline or border, click No Outline.

- Click a Theme Color or Standard Color to apply it to the outline or border.

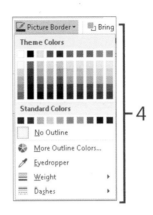

> **TIP** The Arrow option on the Shape Outline or Picture Border palette is available only if you are working with a line object.

Apply a shape effect

1 In the Slides pane, click an object in a slide to select it.

2 Depending on the type of object you selected, click either the Picture Tools|Format or Drawing Tools|Format contextual tab.

(continued on next page)

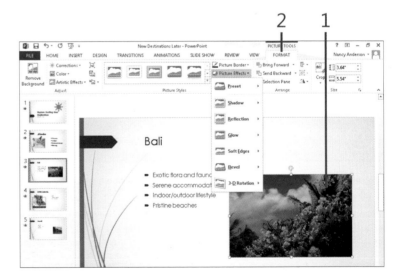

Apply a shape effect *(continued)*

3 In the Picture Styles group, click the Picture Effects button. (Or, in the Shape Styles group, click the Shape Effects button, again, depending on what you've selected in the slide.)

4 Move your mouse pointer over a category of effects and then click an effect in the gallery that appears.

5 Repeat steps 3 and 4 to apply additional effects to the object.

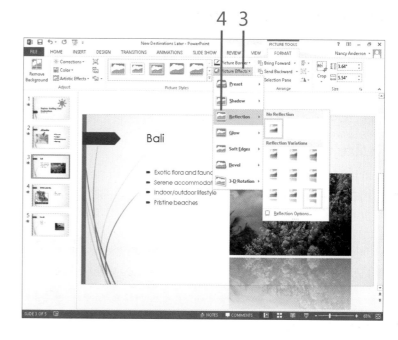

TIP You can apply more than one effect to an object. For example, you might choose to add a shadow, a reflection, and a 3-D effect to one image. Just remember that you have to apply these effects one by one, using the steps outlined here.

TRY THIS Click the Format Shape dialog box launcher in the Shape Styles group to open the Format Shape pane. From there you can apply all kinds of effects to the selected object from one place. When you are done applying effects, click the pane Close (X) button.

Resizing and deleting objects

When you insert an object in PowerPoint 2013, it might not fit exactly as you'd like alongside other objects or placeholders on your slide. In that case, you can resize the object easily by using the resizing handles that appear when you click the object. Dragging corner handles resizes the object while maintaining its original proportions. Dragging handles on the sides of the object resizes it but does not maintain the original proportions. This can cause it to appear somewhat distorted (your object might look stretched or squished), like the image in a funhouse mirror. You also can delete unwanted objects at any time.

Resize objects

1 In the Slides pane, click an object that you want to resize.

2 Drag one of the corner sizing handles inward to shrink the object proportionally or drag outward to enlarge it.

3 To resize the object to a specific measurement, click the Drawing Tools|Format or Picture Tools|Format contextual tab.

4 In the Size group, in the Shape Height and Shape Width boxes, specify a measurement.

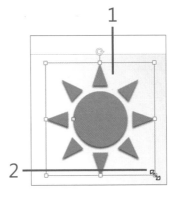

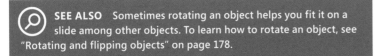

SEE ALSO Sometimes rotating an object helps you fit it on a slide among other objects. To learn how to rotate an object, see "Rotating and flipping objects" on page 178.

TIP If a picture is too large for your slide, consider cropping it by using the Crop tool in the Size group on the Picture Tools|Format contextual tab. With this tool, you can trim out unneeded portions of the picture, thereby saving space, without reducing the picture size, which might make it hard to see. For more about cropping a picture, see "Crop a picture" on page 154.

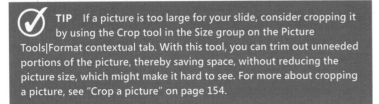

Delete objects

1 In the Slides pane, click an object that you want to delete.

2 Press the Delete key on the keyboard.

If the object was in a slide layout placeholder, the placeholder reappears after you delete the object.

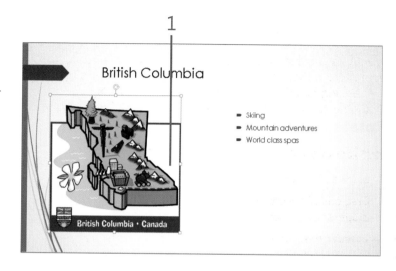

The placeholder reappears after you delete the object.

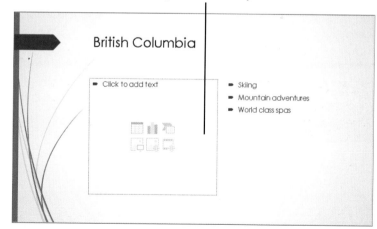

✓ **TIP** You also can use the Cut and Paste choices in the Clipboard group on the Home tab to move a picture from one slide to another. This can save time if the graphic is an online picture that you've previously downloaded and don't want to download again.

Rotating and flipping objects

Being able to rotate objects helps you make making interesting design arrangements on your slides, or it can help you to organize objects so that they fit together. Rotating is easy to do: simply use the rotation handle that appears whenever you click an object. By dragging the handle, you can rotate the object to any point about a 360-degree axis.

Rotate an object

1 In the Slides pane, click the object to select it. A round rotation handle appears, centered above the object.

2 Drag the rotation handle to rotate the object. The mouse pointer changes to a circle of arrows when you're rotating the object. When the object appears at the angle you want, release the mouse button.

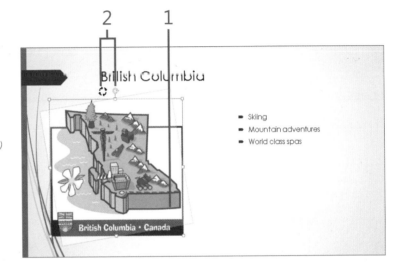

(continued on next page)

SEE ALSO   You can apply 3-D rotation effects to give objects perspective—as if they were rotated to place one edge farther in space from you than the other. To learn how to apply 3-D effects, see the task "Apply a shape effect" on page 174.

Rotate an object *(continued)*

3 To rotate the selected object precisely 90 degrees, click the Home tab.

4 In the Drawing group, click the Arrange button.

5 In the list that appears, point to Rotate.

6 From the submenu that opens, choose Rotate Right 90° or Rotate Left 90°.

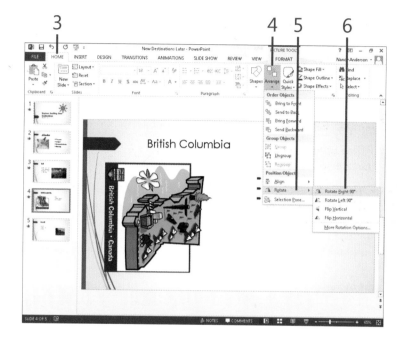

TIP For more rotation options, on the Rotate menu, click More Rotation Options. In the Format Picture pane that opens, in the Size choices, you can enter specific measurements for height and width as well as for setting the distance of the object from the edges of the slide.

Flip an object

1 In the Slides pane, click the object to select it then, on the ribbon, click the Home tab.

2 In the Drawing group, click the Arrange button.

3 In the list that appears, point to Rotate. From the submenu that opens, choose Flip Vertical or Flip Horizontal.

The action is previewed on the slide.

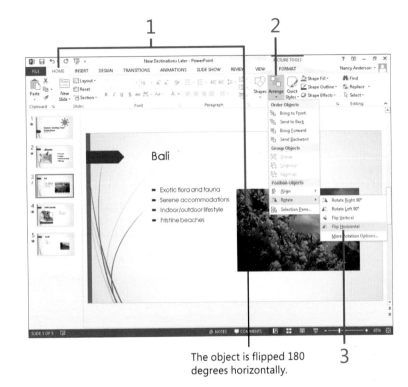

The object is flipped 180 degrees horizontally.

TIP Flipping shifts the object precisely 180 degrees and creates a mirror image. To precisely place an object on your slide without creating a mirror image, use the rotation handle to manually rotate it. Display gridlines so that you can align the object precisely to the edge of the slide and not at an angle. To display gridlines, click the View tab and select the Gridlines check box in the Show group.

Grouping and ungrouping objects

In PowerPoint 2013, when you group several objects together you can manipulate them as if they were a single object. You can then work with that single object to format, move, or resize it. You also can ungroup a grouped object when you no longer need the grouping.

Group and ungroup objects

1 In the Slides pane, click an object to select it.

2 Press Ctrl and then click one or more additional objects that you want to group together.

(continued on next page)

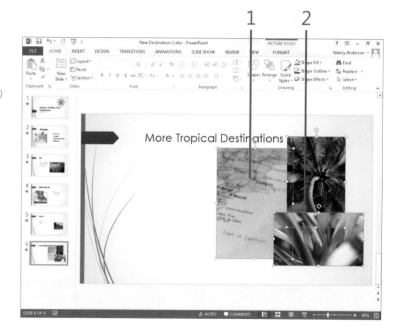

Group and ungroup objects (continued)

3 Click either the Drawing Tools|Format contextual tab or Picture Tools|Format contextual tab, depending on the type of object you've selected.

4 In the Arrange group, click the Group Objects button.

5 On the drop-down list, click Group.

6 To ungroup the objects, select the grouped object, click the Group Objects button, and then click Ungroup.

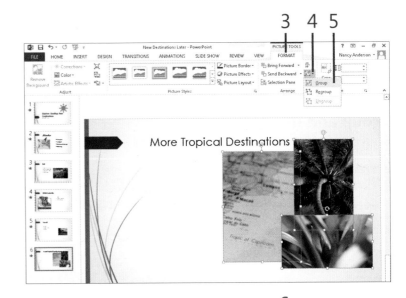

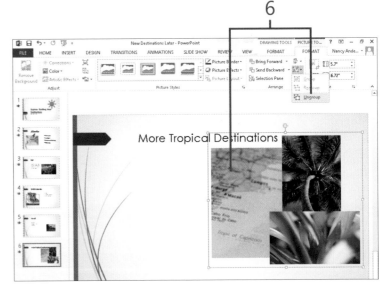

> **TIP** A grouped object has one outline surrounding all the objects and a single rotation handle. After objects are grouped, you can resize, move, rotate, and change the fill color of all the objects at once.

Changing the order of and merging objects

You might want to have several objects on a slide overlap one another, either to save space or to create a design effect. In that case you should know how to control the order of objects on a page—that is, which object appears on top and which appears to be positioned underneath another. You also can take advantage of the new Merge Shapes feature to combine shapes into an interesting new object based on how the individual shapes overlap.

Change object order

1 In the Slides pane, click an object to select it.

2 Click either the Picture Tools|Format contextual tab or Drawing Tools|Format contextual tab, depending on the type of object with which you're working.

(continued on next page)

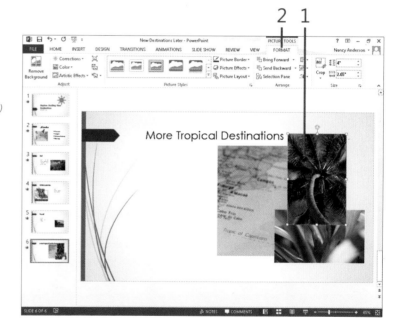

Change object order *(continued)*

3 In the Arrange group, click the Bring Forward button or Send Backward button to move the object one layer forward or backward within the series of objects it overlaps.

If you want to move an object all the way forward or backward in a stack of objects, rather than moving it one position at a time, you can click the arrow on either the Bring Forward or Send Backward button and choose Bring To Front or Send To Back.

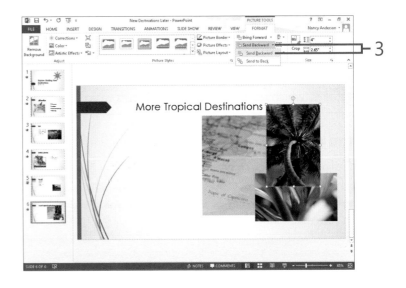

SEE ALSO For more information about inserting objects on your slides, see Section 10, "Inserting media and drawing objects," starting on page 127.

Merge objects

1 Create and format a number of shapes or pictures and arrange them to make a more complex graphic.

2 Press Ctrl and click each of the shapes or drag over them to select them all.

3 Click the Drawing Tools|Format contextual tab.

4 In the Insert Shapes group, click the Merge Shapes button and move your mouse pointer over the various merge choices to see them previewed on the selected shapes.

5 Click a merge choice to apply it.

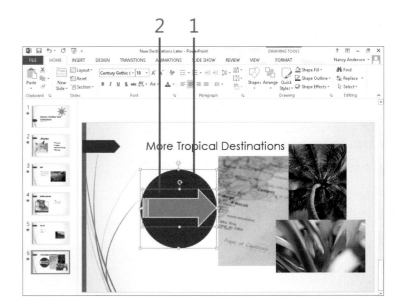

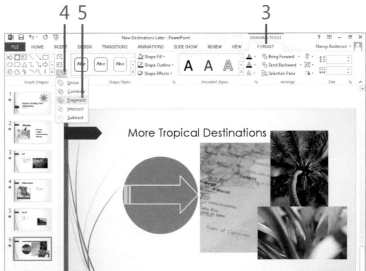

Working with picture tools

Because pictures have attributes such as brightness and contrast, they have their own special set of tools to make adjustments to them. By using these tools, you can make pictures that are too dark appear brighter, and pictures that are hard to see crisper by adjusting the contrast between darks and lights. You can also recolor pictures to apply a wash of light or dark color to them.

Adjust brightness or contrast

1 In the Slides pane, click a picture to select it.

2 Click the Picture Tools|Format contextual tab.

3 In the Adjust group, click Corrections.

(continued on next page)

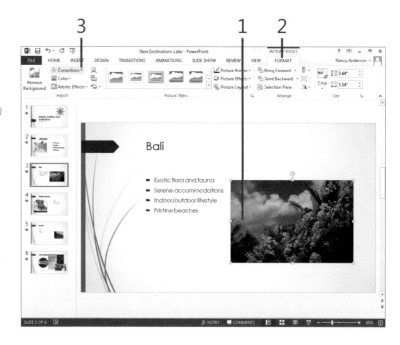

TIP If you want to explore some interesting effects for your picture, such as adding granularity to the photo or washing away details to make it appear more like a drawing, click the Artistic Effects button, move your mouse pointer over the effects displayed to preview them, and then click the desired effect.

Adjust brightness or contrast *(continued)*

4 In the Brightness/Contrast section or the Sharpen/Soften section of the Corrections gallery, choose an option. The effects are previewed on the picture as you move your pointer over each effect.

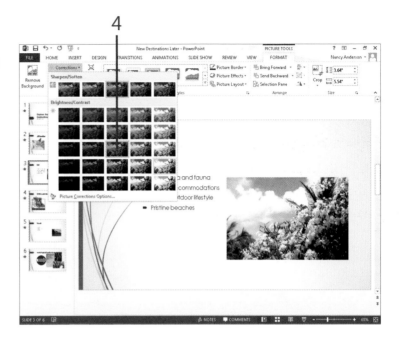

TIP The Photo Album feature was introduced in PowerPoint 2007. You use it to create groups of photos to help you organize your images. For more about Photo Album, see "Creating a photo album" on page 159.

Recolor a picture

1 In the Slides pane, click a picture to select it.

2 Click the Picture Tools|Format contextual tab.

3 In the Adjust group, click the Color button.

The Color gallery opens.

4 Move your pointer to any Color Saturation, Color Tone, or Recolor option to preview it.

5 Click an option to apply it.

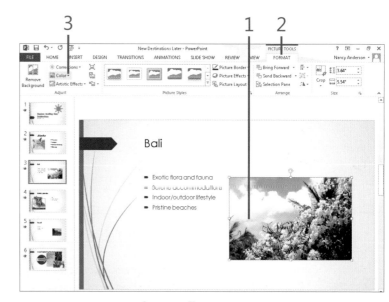

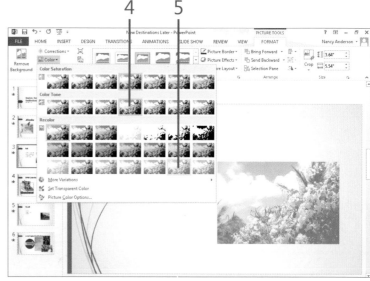

> **TIP** When you click Set Transparent Color on the Color gallery, the portion of the image that you drag over with your mouse disappears, revealing any objects underneath.

> **CAUTION** Be careful how you recolor pictures. Although coloring a picture can add some interest, it can also make the picture difficult to see in certain settings. Consider instead applying a colored border or slide background to add visual interest to a picture.

Using video tools

Not to be left behind in the age of video sharing sites such as YouTube, PowerPoint 2013 now offers enhanced video formatting tools. Video is a great way to add some multimedia punch to a presentation. After you insert a video into a presentation, you can use these tools to format the shape and border of your video, modify playback options such as how playback is initiated, or even trim the video to edit out unwanted footage. (For more about inserting video clips, see Section 10, "Inserting media and drawing objects," starting on page 127.)

Apply video formats

1 In the Slides pane, click a video object to select it.

2 Click the Video Tools|Format contextual tab.

3 In the Video Styles group, click the More arrow at the right of the Video Styles gallery.

4 Move your mouse pointer over the styles to preview them on your video clip. When you find one that you like, click it.

(continued on next page)

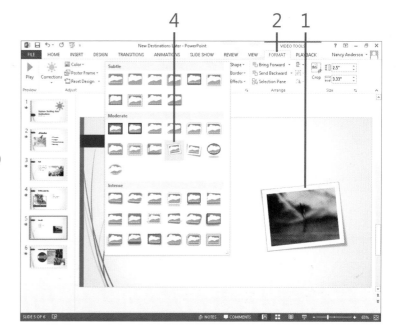

Apply video formats (continued)

5 In the Video Styles group, click the Video Border tool and select a color from the list to change the color of the border.

6 In the Video Styles group, click the Video Effects button, click a category, and then choose from the variety of effects offered there.

5 —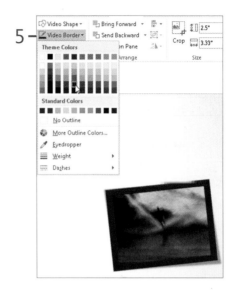

6 —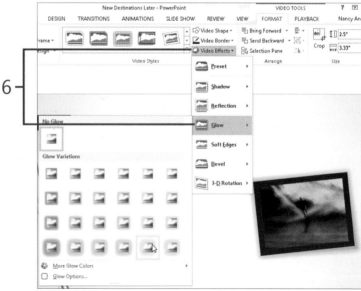

> ✓ **TIP** You can use the Corrections and Color buttons in the Adjust group on the Video Tools|Format contextual tab to modify the appearance of your video. These work similarly to the same tools covered under the previous task, "Working with picture tools."

Set up video playback

1 In the Slides pane, click a video object to select it.

2 Click the Video Tools|Playback contextual tab.

3 In the Video Options group, click the arrow on the Start field. Choose whether the video should play automatically when you display the slide, or manually when you click the video object.

4 Select various check boxes to set whether to play the video in full-screen mode, loop the video to play continuously, or rewind the video after it finishes playing.

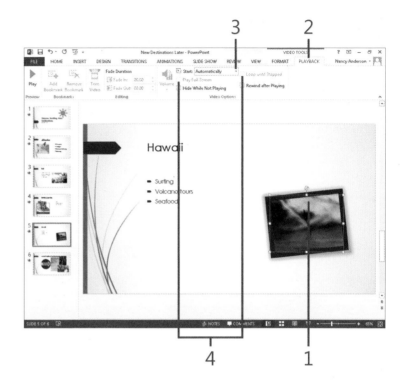

TIP If you want to trim the video to cut some of the footage from it, on the Video Tools|Playback contextual tab, in the Editing group, click the Trim Video button and drag the left or right side of the bar at the bottom of the Trim Video dialog box to cut time from the beginning or end of the video. Click OK to save the changes.

Adding transitions and animations

12

You use animations in Microsoft PowerPoint 2013 to transition from one slide to another when you are showing a presentation in Slide Show view. You can also apply them to individual objects to cause them to appear on a slide using an effect such as spinning or appearing to grow on the slide.

The transition that occurs when you move from one slide to another in a slide show can vary for each slide change or be applied globally. You can also control the speed of each transition, and you can even add a sound to play along with the transition effect.

Using a custom animation effect to control how individual objects are displayed on your slides gives you the ability to have individual bullet points appear in a timed sequence or one by one as you click your mouse. You can even apply a motion path so that an object enters from a certain direction, moves to one area of the slide, and then moves to another, and so forth. PowerPoint 2013 includes Animation Painter, a convenient tool with which you can copy an animation effect or set of effects from one object to another.

Animations and transitions are a great way to draw attention or add visual interest to your presentation.

In this section:

- Applying a transition
- Adding sound to a transition
- Modifying transition speed
- Choosing how to advance a slide
- Applying a custom animation to an object
- Reordering animations
- Using Animation Painter
- Previewing an animation

Applying a transition

You can use a gallery of preset transitions to apply a visual effect that occurs when a new PowerPoint 2013 slide appears during an onscreen slide show. These transition effects are divided into three rather self-explanatory categories: Subtle,

Exciting, and Dynamic Content. You can apply a different effect between individual pairs of slides or one effect that occurs every time a new slide appears.

Apply a transition scheme to a slide

1 To apply a transition to a particular slide, display that slide.

2 On the ribbon, click the Transitions tab.

3 In the Transition To This Slide group, click the More button in the Transitions gallery.

   The Transitions gallery opens.

(continued on next page)

> **TIP** If you decide that you no longer want to include a slide's transition, select the slide, click the Transitions tab, and then in the Transitions gallery, click None (the first item in the Subtle category).

> **TIP** To replay the transition preview, on the Transitions tab, in the Preview group, click the Preview button.

Apply a transition scheme to a slide (continued)

4 Click a transition effect to apply it to that slide. PowerPoint previews the effect.

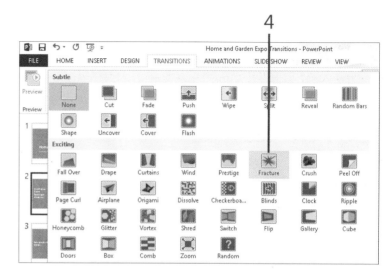

Apply a transition to all slides

1 On the ribbon, click the Transitions tab.

2 Apply a transition scheme to a slide following the steps in the previous task.

3 Click Apply to All.

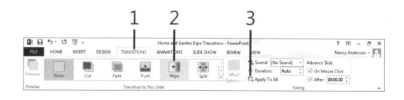

SEE ALSO For more information about adding animations to individual objects on a slide, see "Applying a custom animation to an object" on page 200.

Adding sound to a transition

Imagine that you have applied the Wind transition and changed its options to make the slide appear to blow in from the left side. If you also add the Whoosh or Wind sound effect, you could add impact to the transition. Adding sounds to transitions catches your audience's attention by complementing the transition effect and slide contents. You can also add sounds to custom animations on individual objects—so, when that clip art of a pile of money appears, why not have a cash register sound ring out simultaneously? If you want, you can even add a sound to a slide that doesn't have a transition applied.

Add sound

1 Select a slide that has a transition applied to it. Then, on the ribbon, click the Transitions tab.

2 In the Timing group, click the Sound drop-down arrow.

3 In the drop-down list that appears, click a sound to apply it to the current slide.

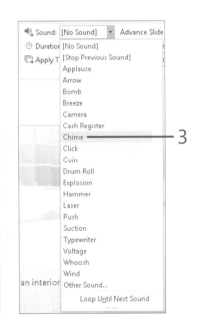

> **SEE ALSO** You can apply a sound to an object that has a custom animation applied to it simply by selecting the object before applying the sound. To learn more, see "Modify animation settings" on page 202.

> **TRY THIS** If you want a previously applied sound to keep repeating until the next sound is played, at the bottom of the Sound drop-down list, click the Loop Until Next Sound option. Repeating a sound in this way can be a great effect, but don't let it go on too long, or you'll drive your viewers crazy!

Modifying transition speed

You can set your PowerPoint 2013 transitions to occur at various speeds. Fast transitions between slides provide a little subconscious shift, but it's so fast that most people don't notice the effect. Transitions that happen slowly, on the other hand, are more noticeable to viewers, but you run the danger of slowing down your presentation if you overuse them. The ability to control the speed of transitions is useful, but you need to determine which speed best fits each transition and your presentation.

Set the speed for transitions

1 Display a slide that has a transition applied to it.

2 Click the Transitions tab.

3 In the Timing group, use the spinner arrows on the Duration field to set the transition to a longer or shorter time.

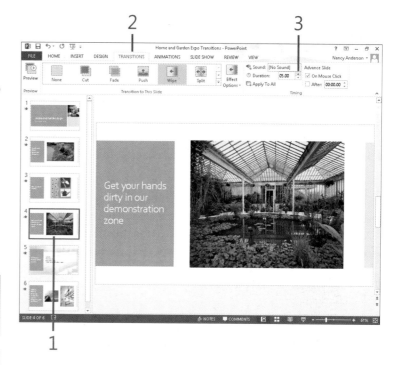

> **SEE ALSO** For information about setting the speed for custom animations applied to individual objects, see "Applying a custom animation to an object" on page 200.

> ⚠ **CAUTION** If you play a sound along with a transition and you set the transition to run fast, the sound occurs quickly, too. In fact, the sound might be so quick that it can be hard to tell what it is. If you associate a sound like a typewriter, for example, with a fast transition, your viewers might hear a single click of a typewriter key—not enough to know what it is they are hearing!

Choosing how to advance a slide

You can advance from slide to slide in a presentation in several ways, such as by clicking your mouse or by waiting for a certain interval of time to pass. The manual approach of clicking your mouse gives you control, but it keeps your hands busy during the presentation. The automatic timed-advance feature is useful when you are showing a slide show on the web or in an unattended setting, such as a mall kiosk. If you need a combination of methods within a presentation, you can make this setting on a slide-by-slide basis by using tools on the Animations tab. You also can apply an effect to the slide animation to control the direction for the transition.

Select a method to advance a slide

1   Display a slide that has a transition applied to it. On the ribbon, click the Transitions tab.

2   To advance slides manually, in the Timing group, select the On Mouse Click check box.

3   Clear the On Mouse Click check box to advance the slide according to preset timings.

4   Use the After box to set a time interval.

    When you play a slide show you now move from one slide to the next after the first slide has been displayed for the specified time interval.

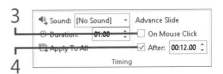

 SEE ALSO   For more about navigating through a slide show presentation, see "Navigating in a slide show" on page 230.

TIP   You can set up your show so that all slides are advanced by using the same method. After making choices as just described, on the Transitions tab, in the Timing group, click Apply To All.

Apply a transition effect

1 Display a slide that has a transition applied to it. On the ribbon, click the Transitions tab.

2 In the Transition To This Slide group, click the Effect Options button.

3 In the drop-down list that appears, click a direction to apply it to the current slide's transition.

A preview of the transition plays.

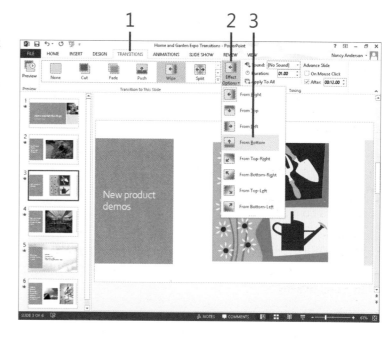

TIP As you adjust the various settings, remember that you can use the Preview button in the Preview group on the Transitions tab to play the transition with the current settings.

Applying a custom animation to an object

You can apply animations to individual objects on your Power-Point 2013 slide, from clip art and pictures to text placeholders. Animations include effects that make an object seem to appear on or disappear from your slide in Slide Show view according to a preset animation effect. For example, you might choose to have a heading appear letter by letter or fly onto your slide. You can use the Motion Path category of animations to have the object appear and then move along a path that you specify on your slide .

Add an animation effect to an object

1 Click the object or text placeholder to select it.

2 Click the Animations tab.

3 In the Advanced Animation group, click Add Animation.

The Animation gallery opens.

(continued on next page)

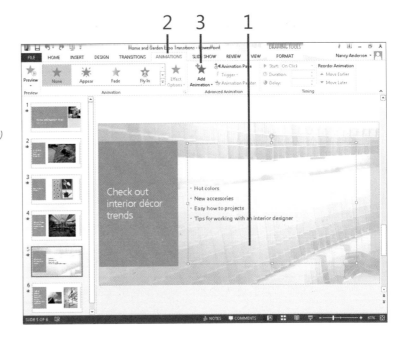

TRY THIS If you want the same animation applied to all objects of a certain type—for example, to all title objects on slides using the Title And Content layout—apply the custom animation in Slide Master view.

Add an animation effect to an object *(continued)*

4 Click an effect in the gallery.

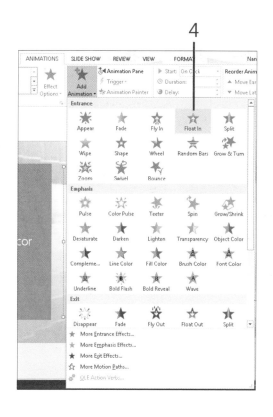

Modify animation settings

1 Display a slide that has an object with an animation effect applied to it.

2 Click the Animations tab.

3 In the Advanced Animation group, click the Animation Pane button to display the Animation pane.

4 In the Animation pane, click the arrow at the right side of the animation that you want to modify in the list. (To expand the list of animations first, if needed, click the bar with the double down-arrow.) A menu of effects settings appears.

5 Click any of the first three settings on this menu to specify whether the effect plays when you click your mouse, along with any previous animation, or after the previous animation.

6 Click the Effect Options command on this menu to open a dialog box specific to the selected effect.

(continued on next page)

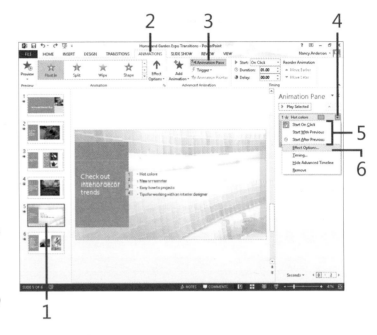

> **TIP** In the Effect Options dialog box, if you select the option of starting an animation after another animation plays, on the Timing tab in this dialog box, then you can specify a delay between the two animations.

Modify animation settings *(continued)*

7 On the Effect tab of the dialog box, you can make certain set-tings, depending on which effect you chose. For example, if your effect animates your text, the Animate Text drop-down list lets you choose to animate by word or by letter.

8 Click the Timing tab. Choose the start setting and duration for the effect and whether it should repeat.

9 Click OK.

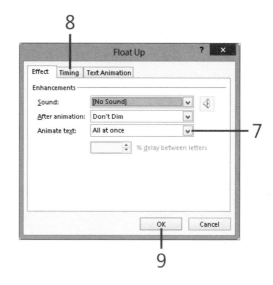

TIP   To remove an animation effect from an object, in the list of effects in the Animation pane, click the arrow next to the animation and click Remove.

Reordering animations

You can use the Animation pane in PowerPoint 2013 to change the order in which animated objects appear during the slide show. For example, for the title slide at the beginning, you might want the title and subtitle to appear before any picture or logo on the slide.

Reorder effects

1 On the Animations tab, in the Advanced Animation group, click the Animation Pane button to display the Animation pane. Then, click an object in the list of animations.

2 Click the up-arrow to the right of Play From to move the effect up in the list.

3 Click the down-arrow to move the effect down in the list.

4 Repeat steps 1, 2, and 3 to reorganize the list of effects in any way you like.

> **→** **TRY THIS** To close the Animation pane, click its Close (X) button. Or, on the Animations tab, in the Advanced Animation group, click the Animation Pane button again.

> **✓** **TIP** If you reorganize slides, remember to check each animation's Start setting. For example, if you want a slide title to use a certain entrance effect that relates to the contents of the slide before it, you might want to change the entrance effect to be relevant to its new predecessor when you move that slide.

Using Animation Painter

You can copy multiple PowerPoint 2013 animation effects from one object and apply them to another single object by using Animation Painter. This popular, time-saving feature was added in PowerPoint 2010, and it works similarly to Format Painter, with which you can copy formats such as font and font color from one piece of text to another.

Copy animations by using Animation Painter

1 Click to select an object that has an animation applied to it.

2 Click the Animations tab.

3 In the Advanced Animation group, click Animation Painter.

4 If the object to which you want to apply the effect is on another slide, go ahead and switch to that slide. The effect remains "loaded" in the Painter while you navigate.

5 Click the object to copy all animation effects from the first object to the second.

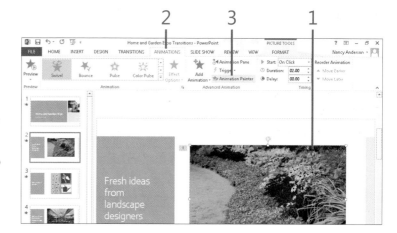

> **TIP** When you click Animation Painter once, you can copy animation effects to one object. If you want to copy the animation effects to more than one other object, double-click the Animation Painter button in step 2. When you finish copying the effect to all the objects that you want, press the Esc key or click the button again to turn off Animation Painter.

Previewing an animation

PowerPoint 2013 offers a couple of options for previewing an animation effect on a slide in Normal view. There is a Preview button on the Animation tab that plays all the effects on a slide, and the Animation pane offers a Play button to play the individual animations on the animation list.

Preview animations

1 With a slide containing animations displayed, click the Animations tab.

2 In the Preview group, click the Preview button to play all animations on the slide.

3 Click Animation pane.

4 Click Play All to play the applied animations in sequence.

5 To stop the preview from running, click the Stop button in the Animation pane at any time.

6 Click the Close (X) button to exit the Animation pane.

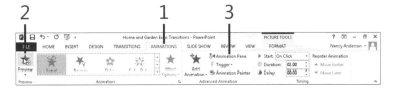

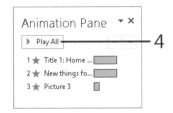

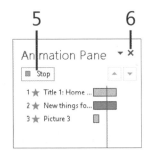

> **TIP** To view the animation in Slide Show view, click the Slide Show button on the status bar near the lower right of the PowerPoint window.

> **TRY THIS** If you click the Play button in the Animation pane to preview the animations, a small timer bar appears at the bottom of the list. This timer tallies up the seconds it takes for all your animations to play.

Finalizing your slide show

13

After you put in all the effort to build a stunning presentation—composing the perfect content and choosing attractive design elements and graphics—you should take the time to proofread it to ensure that you haven't made spelling or other errors. Microsoft PowerPoint 2013 provides a spelling checker to help you check your contents. There's also an available thesaurus to help you find the perfect word. Additionally, you can get feedback about the presentation from other people, who can comment on any problems in the presentation before you deliver it in front of an audience.

At this point you should also set up how you want your slide show to run. For example, will you use multiple monitors, and will the presentation run in a continuous loop or just one time from beginning to end? This is also the time to rehearse your presentation to ensure that the slide show runs smoothly. While rehearsing a presentation, you can add a narration and timings that control how long each slide is displayed. These are useful if the presentation runs on its own with no speaker present.

In this section:

- Checking your presentation's spelling
- Selecting the right word by using the Thesaurus
- Working with comments
- Choosing the slide show type and options
- Choosing slides and an advance method
- Rehearsing your presentation
- Saving rehearsal timings
- Taking a presentation with you
- Sending a presentation by email for review

Checking your presentation's spelling

When you finish adding the last sentence of text and the final graphic objects to your presentation, you're still not quite done. Because your presentation is likely to be displayed on a large screen in front of many people, any error or glitch is likely to undermine the credibility of your message. For that reason, taking the time to check spelling, word choices, and the appearance of your content is very important. PowerPoint 2013 provides tools to help you check the accuracy of your contents.

Check spelling

1 Open the presentation that you want to review. If you want to check the spelling of a single word, select that word.

2 On the ribbon, click the Review tab.

3 In the Proofing group, click Spelling.

   The Spelling pane opens and highlights the first misspelling.

(continued on next page)

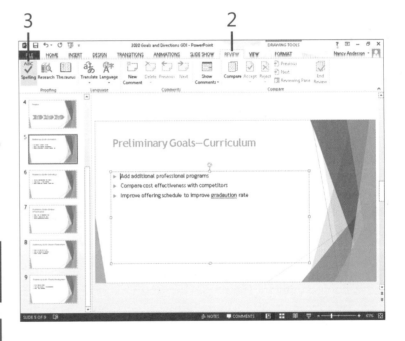

SEE ALSO   For information about viewing and moving slides around in your presentation, see "Navigating slides in Normal view" on page 108 and "Duplicate and move slides" on page 111.

TIP   After working on your presentation for hours, days, or weeks, you are often too familiar with it to spot problems. In addition to using PowerPoint's spelling checker, try to have someone objective read through the presentation, or, if nobody else is available, read each sentence backward yourself to proof it. When we read a sentence forward, we make assumptions about the next word based on context. When we read from the last word to the first, each word and its spelling stand out, and any missing words might be more obvious.

Check Spelling *(continued)*

4 Take any of the following actions:

- Click a spelling in the list of suggestions and then click Change or Change All to apply it to the current word or to all instances of the word in your presentation, respectively.

- Click Ignore or Ignore All to disregard this instance of the spelling or all instances of it in your presentation, respectively.

- Type the correct spelling, which replaces the misspelled word on the slide, and then click Replace in the pane.

- Click Add to include the spelling in the dictionary in PowerPoint.

5 When you click one of the previous options, PowerPoint moves to the next word that needs checking. When all errors have been checked, PowerPoint displays a pop-up message box to inform you that the spelling check is complete. Click OK.

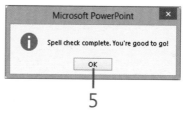

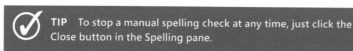

TIP To stop a manual spelling check at any time, just click the Close button in the Spelling pane.

TIP PowerPoint is set up by default to check spelling automatically. This results in wavy colored lines appearing under words that are of questionable spelling. If you right-click one of these words, PowerPoint displays a shortcut menu that offers alternative spellings or words. Just click an entry to make the change.

To hide those wavy lines on your screen if you prefer not to use them to correct spelling, click the File tab, click Options, and then select Proofing. Select the Hide Spelling Errors check box and then click OK.

Selecting the right word by using the Thesaurus

Choosing the right word can help you communicate more effectively. While refining your presentation, you can look for opportunities to change a particular word, either to make your meaning more clear or to reduce repetition in the presentation content. PowerPoint includes a Thesaurus that can suggest words that have similar meanings, which can be very handy when you're not able to think of just the right word.

Use the Thesaurus

1 Display the slide that contains the word you want to check and select that word.

2 On the ribbon, click the Review tab.

3 In the Proofing group, click Thesaurus.

The Thesaurus pane appears on the right side of the screen.

(continued on next page)

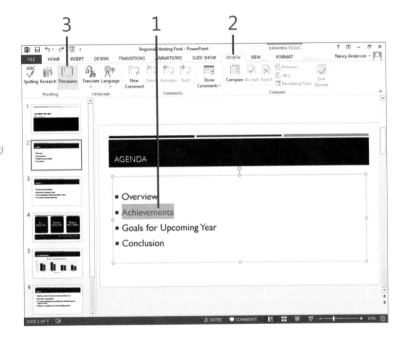

TRY THIS! The Thesaurus also includes antonyms—words with opposite meanings—in its results when one exists for the search word. If you want to say the opposite of a statement such as "This was the best year yet!", enter it on a slide, select the word "best," look it up in the Thesaurus, and then scroll down if needed to find its antonym.

Use the Thesaurus *(continued)*

4 If you want to look up another word instead, select the word currently in the text box and type another word.

5 Click the Start Searching button (the magnifying glass icon on the right of the Search text box).

6 Click a word in the list of results to display additional similar words.

7 Click the Back button to move back to a previous list of words.

8 Click the down-arrow next to a selected word in the Thesaurus and choose Insert to replace the word selected in your presentation.

9 Click the Close button in the Thesaurus pane.

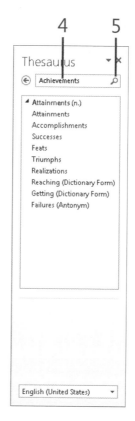

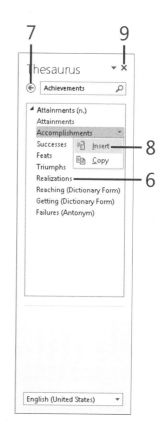

> ✓ **TIP** If you do not want to replace a selected word but instead want to use one of the Thesaurus pane suggestions elsewhere, click the arrow for the word and click Copy. You can then click in a text placeholder on a slide and press Ctrl+V to paste the word into place.

> ✓ **TIP** You can change which language that the Thesaurus uses by clicking the drop-arrow for the language at the bottom of the pane and selecting a different language from the list that appears.

Working with comments

You can send your PowerPoint 2013 presentation to others to review it and ensure that everything looks perfect. You can ask others to make changes or to simply add comments with suggestions for you to review. PowerPoint 2013 features improvements to how comments work, including the ability to respond to and manage comments from within the Comments pane.

Add Comments

1 Display a slide to which you want to add a comment.

2 If you want to attach a comment to a particular object or placeholder, click to select it.

3 On the ribbon, click the Review tab.

4 In the Comments group, click New Comment.

The Comments pane opens. Or, you can open an existing comment as described in the next task to add a reply or new comment for it.

(continued on next page)

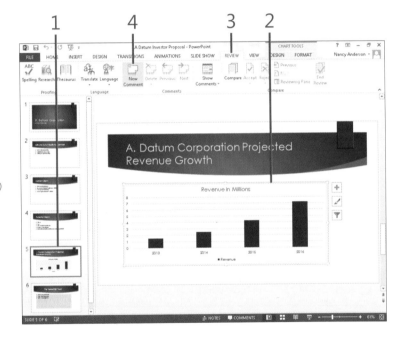

✓ TIP Comments do not show up in Slide Show or Slide Sorter view. They are intended mostly for reviewers to provide feedback or remarks on a presentation as it is being created. If you want to include comments with your presentation, consider adding notes and printing the Notes view for your audience.

Add Comments *(continued)*

5 Click in the text box for the new comment or comment reply, or if you want to add a separate, new comment, click the New button and then, in the new comment that appears in the pane, click in the text box and type your comment. When you're finished, click anywhere outside the comment box.

6 Click the Close button in the Comments pane.

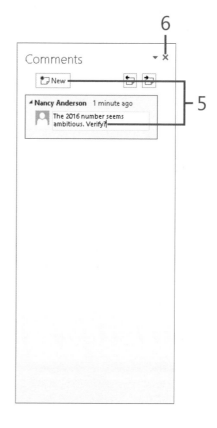

SEE ALSO You can send your presentation by email to colleagues for review by using the Share choice on the File tab. See "Sending a presentation by email for review" on page 224. You also can share a presentation so that colleagues can view it online or download it from your SkyDrive. See "Share a presentation from your SkyDrive" on page 254 to learn more.

Show, hide, and delete comments

1 Click or select a slide that has a comment to review.

2 Click the comment balloon.

   The Comments pane opens.

3 To delete a comment, move the mouse pointer over it and click the Delete button that appears. (If needed, click another comment thread first.)

4 To display comments on other slides for review and removal, in the Comments pane, click the Previous button or Next button.

5 Click the Close button to dismiss the Comments pane.

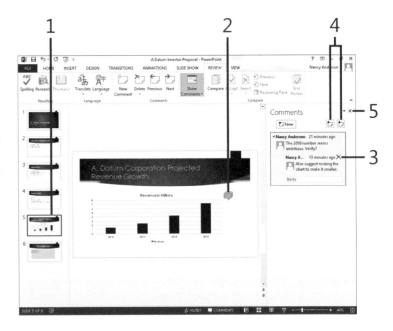

→ **TRY THIS!** Try using the tools in the Comments group on the Review tab to edit, delete, or cycle through comments in your presentation. Click the down-arrow on the Delete button to see choices for deleting all the comments on the current slide or in the entire presentation.

✓ **TIP** Click the Comments indicator on the status bar to show and hide comments. You also can click the Show Comments button in the Comments group on the Review tab to toggle the Comments pane on and off. If you click the down-arrow on the Show Comments button, you can click Show Markup to toggle the display of the comment balloons on and off.

Choosing the slide show type and options

Several variables affect how your slide show runs. For example, you can set up a slide show to be presented by a live speaker or to be browsed by a viewer. You can specify that a show loops continuously or is shown with or without a recorded narration and set animations. You also can choose a pen color in advance to use when you need to annotate the show while presenting it.

Set the show type

1 On the ribbon, click the Slide Show tab.

2 In the Set Up group, click Set Up Slide Show.

The Set Up Show dialog box opens.

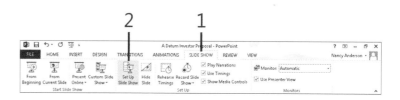

3 In the Show Type section, click one of the three options:

- **Presented By A Speaker** Displays the slide show in Full Screen Mode and assumes a live presenter is running the show.

- **Browsed By An Individual** The setting to use if an individual will view the show from a computer or CD. This option runs the presentation in a window rather than full screen.

- **Browsed At A Kiosk** Provides a self-running, full-screen pre-sentation that will run in a setting such as a trade show booth or store kiosk.

4 Click OK to save your settings.

> **TIP** If you want a show to run unattended, it's a good idea to loop it so that it repeats over and over again in your absence. The task on the next page describes how to turn on looping.

Specify show options

1 Click the Slide Show tab.

2 In the Set Up group, click Set Up Slide Show.

The Set Up Show dialog box opens.

3 In the Show Options section, select any of the three check boxes:

- **Loop Continuously Until 'Esc'** Choose this option if you are running the show unattended and want it to continuously repeat.

- **Show Without Narration** If you recorded a narration but now want a live presenter to give the show, select this option.

- **Show Without Animation** Because animations might not run smoothly on slower computers, you can turn them off by using this setting.

4 To select a color for annotations you can make while running a show, click the down-arrow on the Pen Color list and choose an ink color from the drop-down palette that appears.

5 Click OK to save your settings.

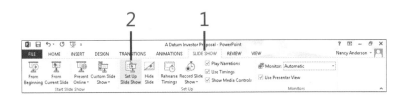

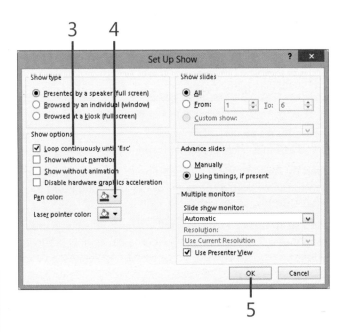

> **TIP** You can choose additional colors for the pen by clicking More Colors at the bottom of the drop-down palette. This displays the Colors dialog box, in which you can select a standard or custom color to apply. You can also use your mouse as a laser pointer during a slide show by holding down Ctrl and pressing the left mouse button. You can set the laser pointer color by using the Laser Pointer Color drop-down palette in the Set Up Show dialog box.

> **SEE ALSO** For information about working with the pen to make annotations during a presentation, see "Make annotations on slides" on page 233.

Choosing slides and an advance method

If you give presentations frequently about a topic but need to tweak each show for the current audience, you can choose to have only a subset of the slides in the presentation included in a particular slide show. In PowerPoint 2013, You can set up your show to advance manually (when a presenter clicks) or automatically according to predetermined timings. Finally, you can specify to use more than one monitor. With this feature, the presenter can use one monitor to orchestrate the show while the audience views the presentation on another monitor.

Specify which slides to include

1 On the ribbon, click the Slide Show tab.

2 In the Set Up group, click Set Up Slide Show.

The Set Up Show dialog box opens.

3 In the Show Slides section, choose one of three options:

- **All**   Choose this to include all slides in the presentation (except the slides you've hidden).

- **From and To Boxes**   Enter the beginning and ending slide numbers here to show a range of slides.

- **Custom Show**   Click this and then select the name of a previously prepared custom show to present different versions of your show to different audiences.

4 Click OK to save your settings.

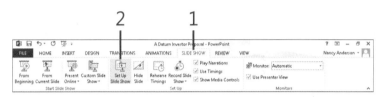

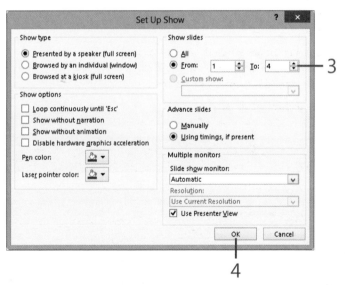

> **TRY THIS!**   If you have a large slide show and find that it's running slowly on the presenting computer, don't shorten your show. Instead, you can modify your monitor's resolution in Windows Control Panel by using the Adjust Screen Resolution link. Your slides run faster at a lower resolution, such as 1024 x 768, although the image quality is grainier.

> **SEE ALSO**   For information about working with custom shows, see "Creating custom shows" on page 265.

Set up slide advance

1 On the ribbon, click the Slide Show tab.

2 In the Set Up group, click Set Up Slide Show.

The Set Up Show dialog box opens.

3 In the Advance Slides section, click an option for how to advance slides:

- **Manually**   Requires you to click a mouse, press an arrow key, or use the navigation tools in Slide Show view.

- **Using Timings, If Present**   Moves the slides forward automatically based on the timings you save when you rehearse the show and save timings.

4 Click OK to save your settings.

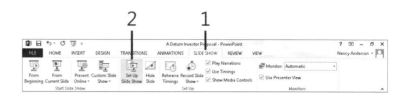

SEE ALSO   For more information about how to move from slide to slide in a presentation, see "Navigating in a slide show" on page 230.

TIP   The Show Presenter View option in the Set Up Show dialog box can come in handy if you have a system with multiple monitors. Select it if you want to control the show from one screen—your laptop, for instance—but use another screen to display the presentation to your viewers. By using the Show Presenter View option on your screen, you can navigate the slide show, and your actions are invisible to your viewers. For example, you can use thumbnails of your slides to build a custom presentation during the show, reordering slides as you go to offer a recap of key ideas.

Rehearsing your presentation

It's very important that you prepare for your presentation. Rehearsing has several benefits. It helps you to spot problems in running your presentation, such as animations that take a long time to play or type that is hard to read. In addition, during rehearsal you can record a narration that can be played for a self-running slide show on CD or a kiosk.

Add a narration

1 Attach a microphone to your computer if one is not built in.

2 On the ribbon, click the Slide Show tab.

3 In the Set Up group, click the down-arrow on the Record Slide Show button and choose Start Recording from Beginning or Start Recording from Current Slide.

The Record Slide Show dialog box opens.

4 Ensure that the check boxes for Slide And Animation Timings and Narrations And Laser Pointer are selected and then click the Start Recording button.

(continued on next page)

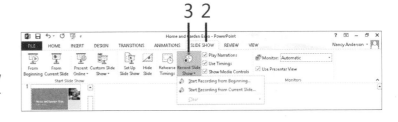

> **TRY THIS!** When you record a narration, you are offered the option of saving timings, as well. If you do, those timings can be used to advance slides based on when the narration for each slide is complete. The Slide Show tab includes a Use Timings check box that you can clear to override narration timings.

> **TRY THIS** You can clear timings you recorded previously by clicking the Record Slide Show button and choosing Clear. On the menu that appears, you can clear timings or narrations on the current slide or for all slides

Add a narration *(continued)*

5 The presentation begins. The Recording toolbar appears in the upper-left corner. Navigate through the presentation, reading your narration into your microphone.

6 To stop recording at any point, click the Close button on the Recording toolbar.

7 On the status bar, click the Slide Sorter button to view the recorded timings and see the narration icon in the lower-left corner of each slide.

6

7

> ✔ **TIP** Your sound quality is better if you have a more sensitive microphone. It might be worth spending a bit more for a better microphone headset to provide quality recording. Typically, an outlet for plugging in a microphone or a headset is on the back or front of your computer, and no other special hardware is required.

Saving your rehearsal timings

After rehearsal, you can save timings that you can then use to advance your slides automatically. This affords you the ability to move about while presenting or play a show unattended.

Save timings

1 On the ribbon, click the Slide Show tab.

2 In the Set Up group, click Rehearse Timings.

3 Navigate through your slide show, displaying each slide for the approximate length of time that you want to display it and discuss its contents.

4 When the slide show is done, in the pop-up message box that displays the total time for the show, click Yes to keep the settings or No to discard them.

5 Click the Slide Sorter view button and note that saved timings appear beneath slides.

> **SEE ALSO** For more information about running your slide show, see the tasks "Navigating in a slide show" on page 230 and "End a show" on page 239.

> **TIP** If you add to or change the content of your presentation in any way, you might want to change the saved timings. To save new timings, simply run the Rehearse Timings feature again and save the timings. Only one set of timings can be saved with your slides.

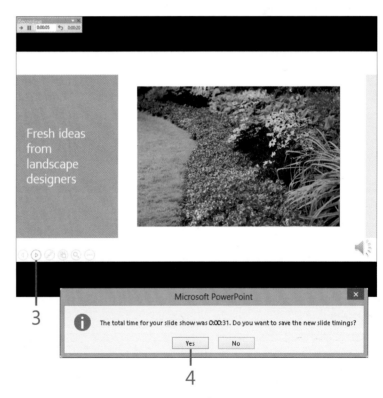

Taking a presentation with you

Most of the time, you don't give a PowerPoint 2013 presentation where you designed it. Instead, you travel with it, whether the locale is a meeting room two doors down or in another state or country. To do this, you save a presentation to media such as a USB flash drive or CD. When you publish your presentation to media in this way, you can use the PowerPoint Web App to run the presentation on a computer that doesn't have PowerPoint installed, although you should test running the presentation in this way first to ensure that all the animations and other features play as you expect.

Save a presentation to portable media

1 Insert a CD or DVD into your computer's CD/DVD drive or insert a USB flash drive into a USB port.

2 On the ribbon, click the File tab to display the Backstage view.

3 Click the Export tab.

4 Click Package Presentation For CD.

5 On the right side of the window, click the Package For CD button.

The Package For CD dialog box opens.

(continued on next page)

TIP You can use the Options button in the Package For CD dialog box to modify how presentations play in the PowerPoint Viewer and to choose whether to include linked files and TrueType fonts. If you want to ensure that the fonts in your presentation display accurately on another computer, select the Embedded TrueType Fonts option in the Options dialog box.

Save a presentation to portable media *(continued)*

6 Enter a name for the CD/DVD.

7 To add more files, such as files that you need for background information, click Add and select them. (You will then be prompted to include linked files after step 8.)

8 If you're using a CD/DVD, click Copy To CD. If you're using a USB drive, click Copy To Folder. In the Copy To Folder dialog box, use the Browse button to select the destination USB and then click OK.

9 Click Yes in the pop-up message box that appears, asking whether you want to include linked files.

Any linked files such as hyperlinked images on your hard drive are copied along with your presentation.

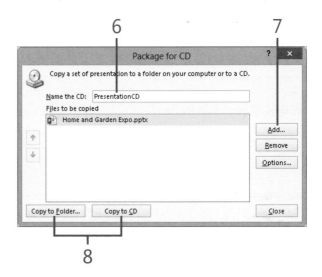

 TIP If you publish your presentation to a flash drive, you can then post the folder on the web or copy it to another computer.

Sending a presentation by email for review

You can send a presentation by email to colleagues for review. They can then use the Comments pane to add their feedback and observations. When you send a presentation by email, it is sent as a file attachment. Each recipient can then save the received presentation.

Send a presentation by email

1 Open the presentation that you want to send via email. Click the File tab to display the Backstage view.

2 Click the Share tab.

3 Click Email and then choose whether to send the file as an attachment, a link, or an XPS or PDF document by clicking one of the buttons in the Email section to the right.

4 In the email message window that opens in your default email program, type a recipient's email address in the To field.

5 Type a subject in the Subject field, if needed.

6 Type the text of any message that you want to send in the body of the message.

7 Click Send.

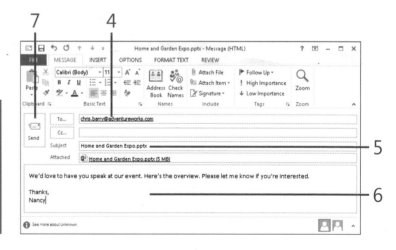

> ✓ **TIP** If you are sending the presentation to somebody who doesn't have PowerPoint available, that person can view it by using PowerPoint Web App (assuming they have a Microsoft account. Or, you could consider saving the presentation as a PDF or an XPS file. These formats retain most formatting on any Windows-based computer; however, viewers cannot use reviewing features such as inserting comments nor can they play the onscreen slide show with animations and transitions and other audio or video.

Running a presentation

14

In this section:

- Starting your slide show
- Using Slide Show view controls
- Navigating in a slide show
- Working with the pen and annotations
- Erasing and saving annotations
- Using presenter view
- Switching programs and ending a show

Now that you have built your slides, set up your slide show, rehearsed your presentation, and saved it to a CD or USB drive, the time has come to present it to an audience. If the show is set up to be given by a live presenter, the presenter must know how to run the show, navigate between slides, annotate slides, and other tasks. (For more about settings for live presentations, see Section 13, "Finalizing your slide show," starting on page 207.)

Microsoft PowerPoint 2013 offers a few different ways to move around a presentation and also a set of annotation tools with which you can make notes as you present. If your presentation sparks interesting ideas, action items, or questions that you need to follow up on, you can use the annotation tools to jot notes and save those annotations with your presentation. You can also switch to another program or even go online while you're presenting to display other kinds of documents and content.

Knowing how to use these tools can make the difference between a smooth presentation and an awkward viewing and presenting experience.

Starting your slide show

Starting a slide show in PowerPoint 2013 involves nothing more than displaying Slide Show view. This view shows your slides in Full Screen Mode (unless you set up your show to be browsed by an individual, in which case your slides appear with a scroll bar around them). Running a custom show makes it possible for you to display a saved subset of the full slide show.

Start a show

1 If you are using some form of LCD display or other display equipment, connect it to your computer and turn it on.

2 Open the presentation that you want to present.

3 Display the slide from which you want to begin the show.

4 On the status bar, click the Slide Show button.

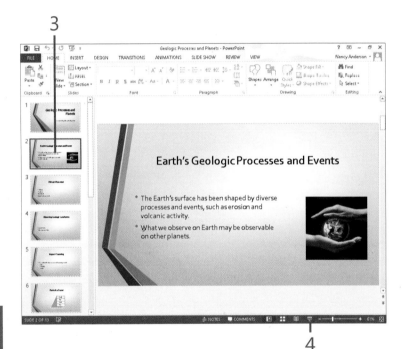

SEE ALSO To learn more about setting up your show to be browsed by individuals or run by a presenter, see "Choosing the slide show type and options" on page 215.

TIP Always try to check your display equipment before you present and, if possible, have the user manual for that equipment handy. In some cases you need to know which button or keyboard combination to use to switch the display on or connect it to your computer.

Start a custom show

1 Open a presentation that contains a custom show.

2 On the ribbon, click the Slide Show tab.

3 In the Start Slide Show group, click the Custom Slide Show button.

4 In the drop-down list that appears, click Custom Shows.

The Custom Shows dialog box opens.

5 Click the custom show title.

6 Click Show.

PowerPoint displays the show in Slide Show view.

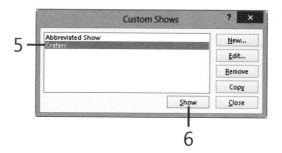

 TRY THIS! If you create a large presentation, create summary slides that introduce each major section of the show. Then, create a custom show that consists of those summary slides. You can go to that custom show at the end of the larger show to review the major topics.

SEE ALSO For information about working with custom shows, see "Creating custom shows" on page 265.

Using Slide Show view controls

When you run a slide show, the controls remain hidden until you need them. This keeps the screen uncluttered so that the audience can focus on your slides and message. When needed, you can display the controls in the lower-left corner of the current slide. PowerPoint 2013 provides a new ability to zoom in on part of the current slide during the show, making it possible for you to show detail in a photo or emphasize data for your audience. The tool for doing that is found in the slide show controls.

Display slide show controls

1 Start the slide show.

2 Move the mouse pointer over the lower-left corner of the slide.

The controls appear.

3 Click the Menu control.

A menu of additional options for working with the show appears.

4 Click outside the menu to close it. Move the mouse away from the controls to fade them from view.

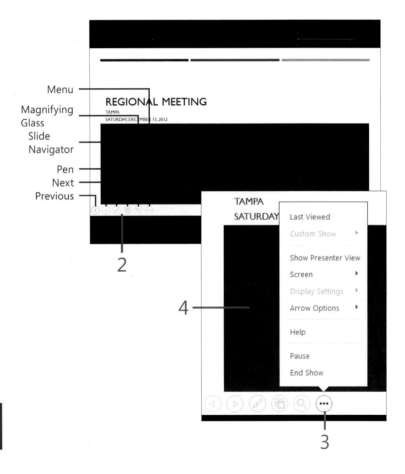

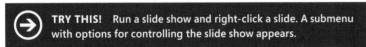

TRY THIS! Run a slide show and right-click a slide. A submenu with options for controlling the slide show appears.

Zoom part of the current slide

1 Start the slide show and go to the slide that you want to zoom.

2 Move the mouse pointer over the lower-left corner of the slide to display the show controls.

3 Click the Magnifying Glass button.

4 Move the mouse pointer over the area that you want to enlarge and then click.

5 Right-click the zoomed slide to return it to its normal size.

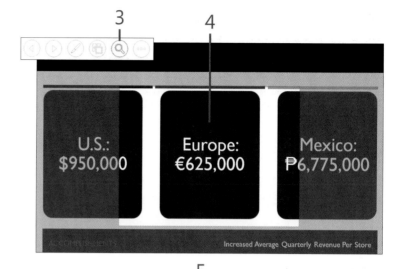

 TIP When a slide is zoomed, you can drag to change the zoomed portion that's displayed.

Navigating in a slide show

Many presenters begin at the first slide in their presentation and move in order to the last slide. But, there are also times when you need to move back to a previous slide to reinforce a point or jump ahead when somebody anticipates a topic through a question or comment. Although I usually offer just the easiest method to get things done in this book, it's very handy for you to learn a few different methods that you can use to navigate from slide to slide.

Move to the next and previous slide

1 Click the Slide Show button in the status bar to display Slide Show view.

2 Use any of these methods to move to the next slide:

- Press the Right Arrow key on your keyboard.
- Click your mouse button.
- In the show controls, click the Next button.
- Press Spacebar on your keyboard.
- Press the Page Up key on your keyboard.

3 Use any of these methods to move to the previous slide:

- Press the Left Arrow key on your keyboard.
- In the show controls, click the Previous button.
- Press Backspace on your keyboard.
- Press the Page Down key on your keyboard.

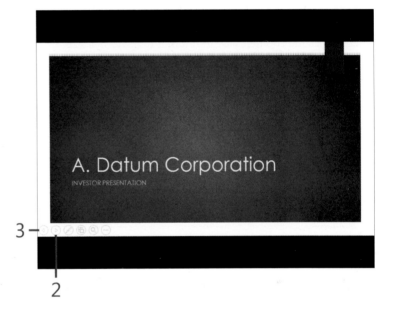

> **TRY THIS!** You can access the Slide Show menu by right-clicking anywhere on your screen while running a slide show. Then, click Next or Previous to move forward or backward in your presentation.

Go to a particular slide

1 In the status bar, click the Slide Show button to display Slide Show view.

2 Move the mouse pointer to the lower-left corner of the slide to display the slide show controls.

3 Click the Slide Navigator button.

4 Click the thumbnail for the slide that you want to display. The slide appears immediately.

3

4

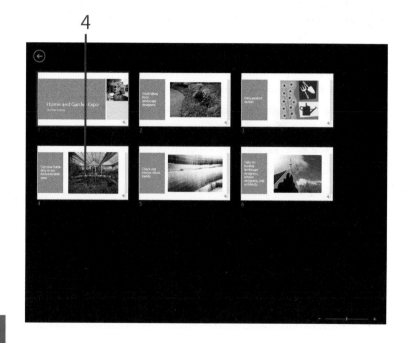

TIP If you know the number of the slide that you want to display, you can press it on the keyboard and press Enter. Or press Ctrl+S to display the All Slides dialog box. Click a slide in the Slide Titles list and click Go To.

TRY THIS! You can display a hidden slide. When you get to the slide before the hidden one, press H, and PowerPoint shows the hidden slide. To return to the previous slide you displayed, click the Slide Show button and choose Last Viewed from the menu that appears.

Working with the Pen tool and annotations

You can use a the Pen tool to take advantage of a Microsoft technology called *ink* to write on your slides when running your presentation in Slide Show view. The Pen tool gives you the option to select different pen types, such as laser pointer, ballpoint, and highlighter, and to change the ink color. You can use the pen to write on slides to take notes while delivering your presentation.

Choose a pen style and color

1 On the status bar, click the Slide Show button to begin the show.

2 Move the mouse pointer to the lower-left corner of the slide to display the slide show controls. Click the Pen button.

3 In the menu that appears, click a pen style to select it.

4 Click the Pen button again.

5 In the menu that appears, click an ink color from the choices located at the bottom of the menu.

> **TRY THIS!** You can also make changes to the arrow pointer that appears when the pen isn't activated. Right-click the slide show, point to Pointer Options, Point to Arrow, and then click Automatic, Visible, or Hidden to specify whether the arrow pointer is visible only when you move the mouse or all the time or if it is invisible.

> **SEE ALSO** If you choose a pen color other than the default to write on a slide, be aware that when you move to another slide, the pen reverts to its default color. For more about choosing a default pen color, see "Specify show options" on page 216.

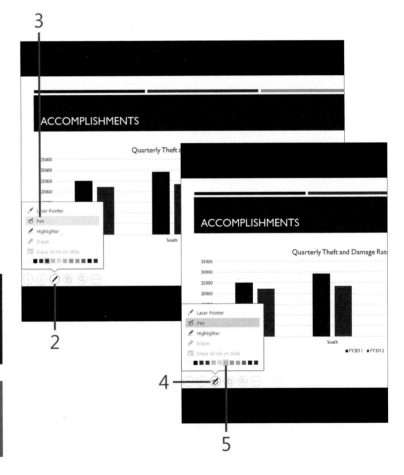

Make annotations on slides

1 With a slide displayed in Slide Show view, display the show controls, click the Pen button, and then choose a pen style.

2 Draw or write wherever you want on the screen by using your mouse. If you chose the highlighter pen style, drag over the object or text that you want to highlight.

3 To turn off the pen, display the show controls, click the Pen button, and then click the current pen style again.

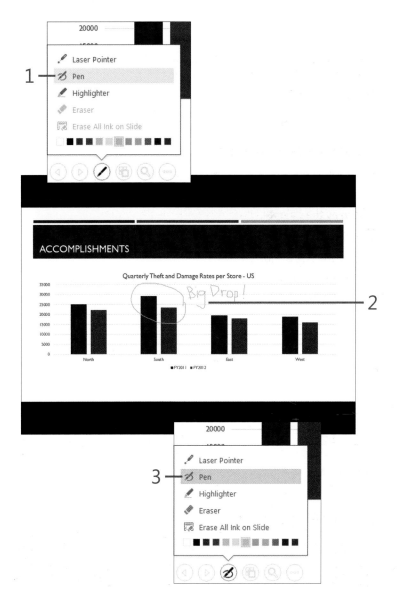

Erasing and saving annotations

After you use the pen to write on slides in PowerPoint 2013, you have two options for how to deal with the annotations. If you no longer need the annotations, you can use an eraser tool to remove the writing, or you can use a command to remove all ink markings on a slide. At the end of your presentation, you are offered the option of saving your ink annotations or discarding them.

Erase annotations on slides

1 Move the mouse pointer to the lower-left corner of the slide to display the slide show controls. Click the Pen button.

2 In the menu that appears, choose Eraser.

3 Move the mouse pointer over the annotation that you want to remove and drag until it disappears.

4 To erase all annotations on a slide, display the show controls, click the Pen button, and choose Erase All Ink On Slide.

5 To turn off the eraser and return to annotating, display the show controls, click the Pen button, and then click a pen type. Or, click Eraser to turn off annotating and erasing.

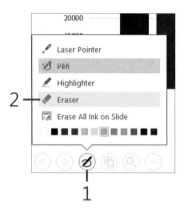

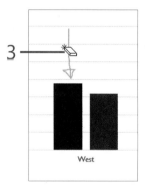

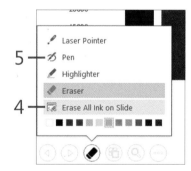

TIP Here are a few shortcuts for turning these tools on and off: to quickly change from the arrow pointer to the Pen tool, press Ctrl+P; to change from the arrow pointer to the Eraser tool, press Ctrl+E; to return to the arrow, press Ctrl+A.

Save annotations

1 Navigate to the end of a presentation in which you've made annotations.

2 When you click to end the show, a message box pops up, asking whether you want to keep ink annotations.

3 Click Keep to save your annotations.

Click Discard if you don't want to save annotations.

4 Saved annotations appear on the slides in Normal view.

TIP After you save an annotation, even if you go back to Slide Show view, you can't use the Eraser tool to erase it. That's because ink annotations are objects that can be resized, rotated, moved, and so on, just like any other object. To remove them from your presentation in Normal view, you can simply click one in the Slides pane and press Delete.

Using presenter view

You can use Presenter view to control a presentation more effectively when you have two monitors connected to the system. When you play a show in Presenter view, your audience sees the typical Slide Show view on one display, and you see the presenter controls on yours. Presenter view also gives you onscreen access to your speaker notes, even though the audience won't see them.

Start a presentation in Presenter view

1 Connect the projector or secondary display equipment to your computer and turn it on.

2 On the ribbon, click the Slide Show tab.

3 In the Monitors group, ensure that the Use Presenter View check box is selected.

4 Start the slide show to display Presenter view on your monitor.

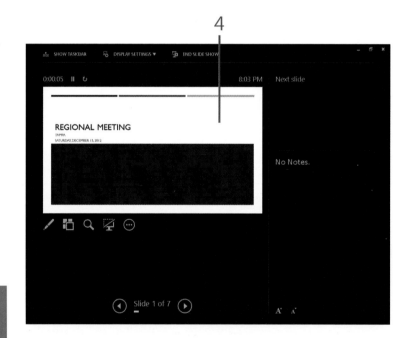

> ✓ **TIP** You can use the From Beginning button in the Start Slide Show group on the Slide Show tab to start the show after you've turned on Presenter view.

Use the Presenter view controls

1 Use the arrow buttons at the bottom of the screen to move among slides.

2 Use the controls under the current slide to annotate, jump to a slide, zoom, toggle a black screen on and off, or display a menu.

3 Look ahead to your next slide by viewing the Next Slide preview.

4 Review your notes for the current slide at the right.

5 Click End Slide Show to finish presenting.

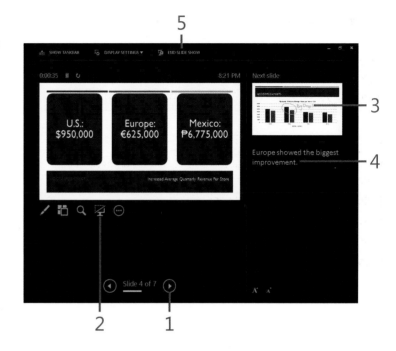

TIP When running a show in the regular Slide Show view, press B to toggle between the slide and a black screen, and W to toggle between the show and a white screen.

TIP Press Alt+F5 to simulate Presenter view when you don't have a second display attached. Practice delivering your full presentation in this view as another rehearsal method.

Switching programs and ending a show

There are many reasons to switch to another program installed on your computer while you are running a PowerPoint 2013 presentation. You might want to demo a software system or run a new product demo in a movie program, or you might want to go to the Internet and browse for information to answer a question. Although you can place links in your presentation that open documents in other programs, if you prefer to open the programs themselves to work in them, you can do so easily. Finally, when you are finished with all of the activities involving your slide show, you should end the show.

Switch to another program

1 With a slide show running and the program to which you want to switch open, right-click the current slide and then, on the shortcut menu that appears, click Screen.

2 On the submenu that opens, click Show Taskbar.

3 On the Windows 8 taskbar that appears, click the program name. Click the thumbnail for one of the open files if multiple open files appear.

4 When you're done working in the program, simply click the Close or Minimize button in the other program.

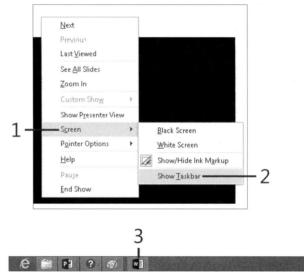

End a show

1 With a presentation running in Slide Show view, do one of the following:

- Press the Esc key on your keyboard.

- Click the Menu button in the show controls and then choose End Show.

- Press Break on your keyboard.

- Press the hyphen key [-] on your keyboard.

- Navigate to the last slide in the presentation and press the Right Arrow key. A black screen appears with a message that instructs you to click to end the show.

2 If you see the end of slide show message, click the message or press Esc on your keyboard.

TIP   Did you forget how to jump to another slide or some other handy navigation shortcut? Don't worry. Display the show controls, click the Menu button at right, and choose Help. A Slide Show Help window appears listing common keyboard commands. This list includes some very useful shortcuts.

Printing a presentation

15

You might choose to print your presentation for any number of reasons. Perhaps you want others to review it to help you correct or edit it before you present your slide show. Or, you might want to print audience handouts or a copy for yourself to refer to while presenting the show. You might also want to preserve a printout of the outline of your contents for your files or to use as the basis for another document.

Whatever your reason for printing your presentation, Microsoft Power-Point 2013 provides tools to help you preview your printed document, add headers or footers, and choose printing options such as page orientation. You can also choose how many slides to print on a page. You can print audience handouts that include several slides on a page and leave space for taking notes. You can also print one slide per page with your speaker notes included. Finally, you can print the Outline view of a presentation, which includes only the outline text.

In this section:

- Displaying information in headers and footers
- Using Print Preview
- Establishing printer and paper settings
- Choosing slides and a print format
- Setting the number of copies and printing

Displaying information in headers and footers

Before you print your PowerPoint 2013 slides, you might want to include information such as the slide number, the date and time the presentation is printed, or the name of the author of the presentation. To do any of these, you use the Header and Footer feature. You can insert separate headers and footers on slides and on notes and handouts. You can also choose to omit header and footer text on the title slide of a presentation.

Insert headers or footers

1 On the ribbon, click the Insert tab.

2 In the text group, click the Header & Footer button.

The Header And Footer dialog box opens.

(continued on next page)

> **SEE ALSO** For information about working with footer placeholders using the Slide Master feature, see "Insert footer information" on page 68.

> **TIP** All items inserted by using the Slide tab in the Header And Footer dialog box are inserted as footers, but you can select and drag the footer placeholders in Slide Master view to place them anywhere on a slide layout as needed. (You also can move them on individual slides, but that is not a good practice because that might break the connection between the slide and its master or theme.) The Notes And Handouts tab offers settings for both header and footer placeholders, and you can move those placeholders around in Handout Master view or Notes Master view.

Insert headers or footers *(continued)*

3 Click either the Slide tab or the Notes And Handouts tab, depending on where you want to set headers and footers.

4 Select the Date And Time check box to include a date and/or time and then choose either of the following options:

- **Update Automatically** Choose this to include the current date and/or time. If you choose this option, use the drop-down lists to select a date/time format, language, and calendar type. The date is updated every time you open the slide show.

- **Fixed** Choose this to include a date you specify by typing it in.

5 Select the Slide Number check box to include the number of each slide.

6 Select the Footer check box and then enter text to appear in the footer.

7 If you are working on the Slide tab, you can select the Don't Show On Title Slide check box to omit the footer information from any slide with a Title Slide layout.

8 Click Apply To All to apply the settings to all slides. On the Slide tab, you have the option to click Apply if you want to apply the settings only to the current slide.

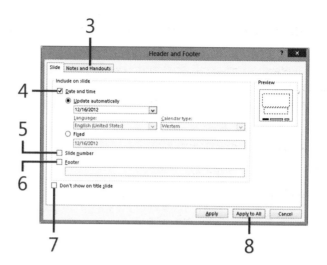

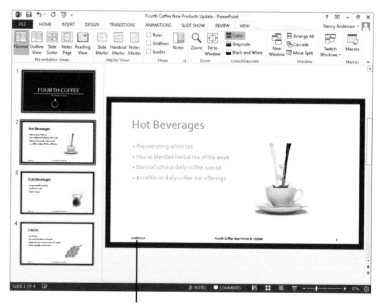

Footers now appear on slides

Displaying information in headers and footers: Insert headers or footers **243**

Using Print Preview

In PowerPoint 2013, Print Preview is included as part of the print options displayed when you choose Print from the Backstage view. It's very useful for previewing documents—including handouts, Outline view, and notes pages—before you print them. Print Preview also offers a zoom slider with which you can view your previews at various sizes.

Display Print Preview

1 On the ribbon, click the File tab to display the Backstage view.

2 Click the Print tab.

The preview appears to the right of the print options.

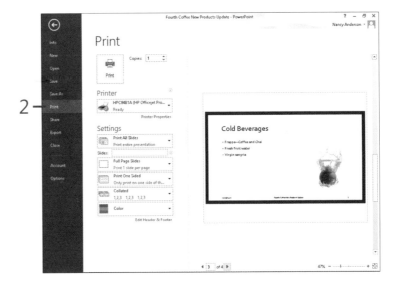

✔ **TIP** Print Preview includes a zoom slider (located in the lower-right corner) that works just like the one in the main PowerPoint window. Use it to enlarge and reduce your preview to review the contents.

🔍 **SEE ALSO** To open Print Preview with a single click, you can add a Print Preview icon to the Quick Access Toolbar. For more information about setting up the Quick Access Toolbar, see "Customizing the Quick Access Toolbar" on page 40.

Navigate Print Preview

1 At the bottom of the Preview pane, click the Next Page or Previous Page button to move forward or backward, one slide or page at a time.

2 In the lower-left corner of the Preview pane, Enter a number in the Current Page indicator and press Enter to display that slide.

3 Click Zoom To Page to adjust the size of the slide to fill the window.

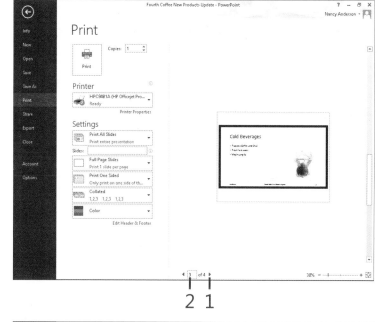

2 1

3

TIP You can choose a percentage at which to display a slide directly in the Zoom dialog box. You can double-click the percentage number on the zoom slider to quickly display the Zoom dialog box in Print Preview.

Establishing printer and paper settings

The PowerPoint 2013 print options include some settings that are probably familiar to you from programs such as Microsoft Word and Microsoft Excel, and some that are specific to Power-Point. Start out by choosing which printer you want to use and changing its printing settings as needed. If you haven't used a Microsoft Office 2013 product before, however, you'll find that print options are accessed a bit differently than in some other programs.

Choose a printer and paper options

1 On the ribbon, click the File tab to display the Backstage view and then click the Print tab.

2 Choose a printer from the Printer drop-down list.

3 Below the selected printer, click the Printer Properties link.

The Properties dialog box for the selected printer opens, showing settings specific to that printer model.

(continued on next page)

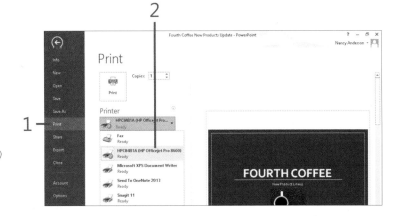

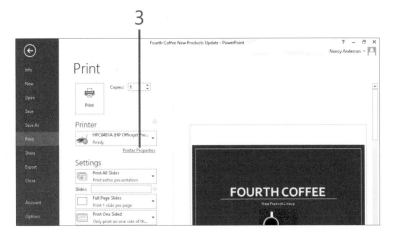

> **✓ TIP** If you want the same printer to be the default option every time you print, in Windows Control Panel (the method for getting there varies depending on whether you are using Windows 7 or Windows 8), go to the Printers And Devices area, right-click a printer, and then choose Set As Default Printer. You can still change the printer when you print an individual file, but that setting applies only to the document you are printing.

Choose a printer and paper options *(continued)*

4 Set the options available for your printer, such as changing the paper size or orientation, keeping in mind that the settings might be found on various tabs. If there is an Advanced button, you can click it to view and use additional printer settings.

5 Click OK to save the settings and return to Print Preview. At this point, you can continue to change the settings as described in the next three tasks or click Print to print your presentation.

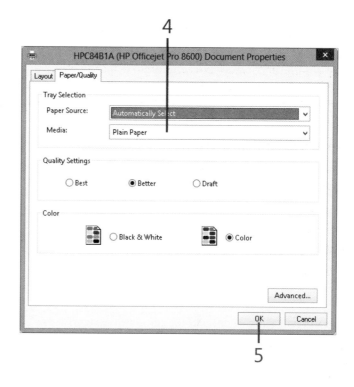

4

5

TIP Different printers offer different property options. For example, if you have a color printer, you can choose to print in color or grayscale. You might be able to select a media type, such as printing to glossy paper or to transparencies for overhead projection. Take a look at Properties dialog box for your printer to see what settings are available to you.

Choosing slides and a print format

Choose which PowerPoint 2013 slides to print and the format in which to print them. For example, you might print the title slide of a presentation to use as a flyer promoting the presentation. You can choose from various formats when printing. You can print slides, the presentation outline, handouts, or notes pages. You can also choose how many slides to include on a single page if you are printing slides, handouts, or notes.

Select the slides to print

1 On the ribbon, click the File tab to display the Backstage view and then click the Print tab.

2 In the Settings section, click the first drop-down list (it initially says Print What) and choose any of the following options:

- **Print All Slides**   Print all the slides in the presentation.

- **Print Selection**   Print whatever contents you select prior to opening the Print settings. Selecting this option limits your navigation in Print Preview to just the selected slides.

- **Print Current Slide**   Print only the currently displayed slide.

- **Custom Range**   Print a range or selection of slides. Enter slide numbers or a range (2, 15, or 3-15, for example).

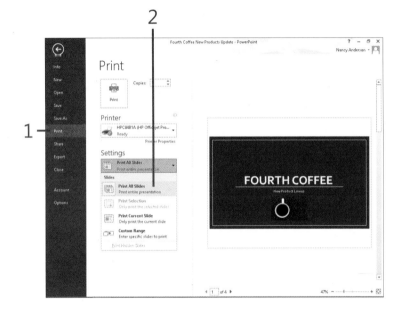

✓ **TIP**   You can click the Print button at any time. You don't need to change all the print settings unless they are necessary for your current print job.

Choose the format to print

1 On the ribbon, click the File tab to display the Backstage view and then click the Print tab.

2 In the Settings section, click the second drop-down list, for specifying the type of output to print. (It initially says Full Page Slides.)

3 Choose the type of output to print. If you select Handouts, click the number of slides per page that you want.

Choose a horizontal option in the Handouts area to print pages with multiple slides progressing from left to right across the page. Click a vertical option to have slides progress down the page along the left margin and then move to the top of the right side of the page in a second column.

4 To add or remove a printed frame around slides, reopen the drop-down list and select or clear the Frame Slides checkbox. (Choosing one of the Handout options frames the slides by default.)

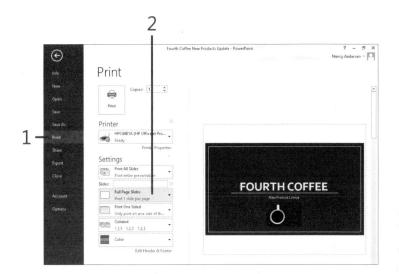

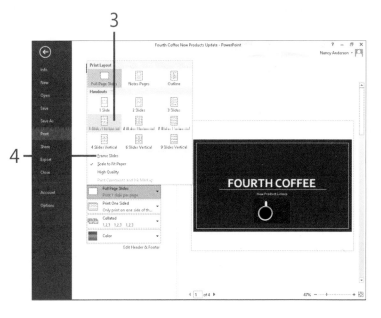

> ✓ **TIP** If you want to prepare a printed outline of your presentation in Microsoft Word rather than in PowerPoint, you can copy the outline from the PowerPoint Outline pane, paste it into Word, and then prepare the outline for printing from Word's Print options.

> 🔍 **SEE ALSO** For more information about working with handouts and notes layouts, see "Working with the handout master" on page 77, and "Working with the notes master" on page 79.

Setting the number of copies and printing

The final print choice that you might need to change is the number of copies to print. If you're printing handouts, chances are you'll need several—one for each of your audience members. After specifying how many copies to print, send the presentation to the printer.

Set the number of copies and print

1 On the ribbon, click the File tab to display the Backstage view and then click the Print tab.

2 In the Copies field, click the spinners up or down as needed until the number of copies you want to print appears or type the number directly in the text box.

3 Use the Collated drop-down list to collate the pages of multiple copies. Use the Print One Sided drop-down list to print on one or both sides of the paper.

4 Click Print.

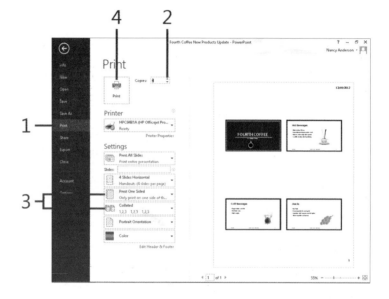

> ✓ **TIP** If you have to print a lot of copies and want to reduce the number of pages, consider modifying the number of slides per page that you print for handouts or notes pages. For more information about this setting, see the task "Choose the format to print" on page 249.

Sharing a presentation

16

The ability to save a presentation to your SkyDrive in the cloud makes it possible for colleagues to review your ideas at any time and from any location that has Internet access. You can, for example, share your presentation as a follow up to giving it in person so that your audience can review or print the content for themselves at their leisure. You might also publish a presentation to the web for others to review and suggest changes before you present it.

You can save a presentation to the web by using your Microsoft ID and placing the file in a public folder on your SkyDrive, and then sharing it from there.

You can broadcast your presentation online to people in a remote location by using Office Presentation Service. The people you invite can open and view your presentation in a web browser.

You can also save files in other formats for sharing. For example, you can save a presentation in PDF format so that anybody can view it by using the free Adobe Reader. This is a handy way to share the file with those who don't have Microsoft PowerPoint, or to share it on the web.

Saving a presentation to the cloud

PowerPoint 2013 works seamlessly with the online SkyDrive storage you receive free with the Microsoft account that you use to sign in to Windows and Office 2013. The basic SkyDrive account provides 7 GB of free storage, more than enough for you to store and share numerous presentations with colleagues.

Saving to your SkyDrive also makes sense if you travel often, because you'll always be able to access your files remotely via an available Internet connection. Note that if you intend to share a presentation from your SkyDrive, you need to place it in a public or shared folder.

Save to your SkyDrive

1 On the ribbon, click the File tab to display the Backstage view.

2 Click the Save As tab.

3 On the Save As screen, in the middle section, click your SkyDrive.

4 Click the Browse button.

The Save As dialog box opens.

(continued on next page)

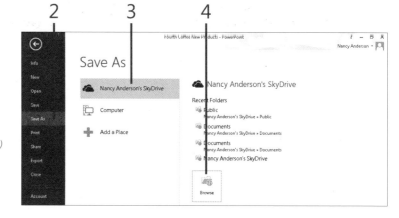

> ✓ **TIP**   As noted in Section 2, to sync your files from your SkyDrive on your hard disk, you need to have the SkyDrive for Windows application installed. This provides the advantage of being able to choose the destination folder on your local and cloud SkyDrive when performing the save. SkyDrive for Windows might be included with your version of Windows 8, but if you need to get it for either Windows 7 or Windows 8, you can go to *https://apps.live.com/skydrive*. Or, sign in at *skydrive.live.com* and click Download if a Get SkyDrive For Windows message appears at the bottom, or click the Get SkyDrive apps link at the bottom of the left pane.

Save to your SkyDrive (continued)

5 If you have SkyDrive for Windows installed, locate the folder on your SkyDrive where you want to save the presentation. To do this, under Favorites, click SkyDrive and then double-click one of the folders that appears.

6 Edit the file name if needed.

7 Click Save.

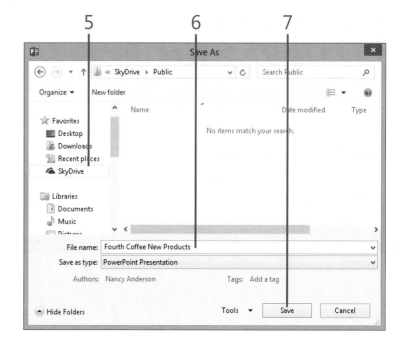

Share a presentation from your SkyDrive

1 Save the file to share to your SkyDrive, as described in the preceding task, but leave the file open in PowerPoint.

2 On the ribbon, click the File tab to display the Backstage view.

3 Click the Share tab.

4 In the Share section, click Invite People.

5 In the Type Names Or E-Mail Addresses text box, type the contact email addresses.

6 Type a message about the shared file, if you want.

7 Click Share.

After SkyDrive sends the invitation, the name of each user with whom you've shared the document appears in the Shared With section at the bottom of the Share screen.

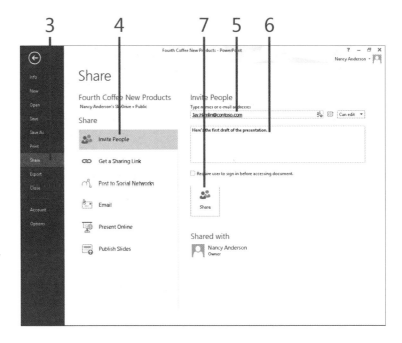

TIP If you click Invite People on the Share screen of the Backstage view and you see a Save To Cloud button, clicking it takes you to the Save As choices, where you need to select your SkyDrive and save to it, as described in the preceding task.

TRY THIS Include your own email address when you use Invite People to share the file. Then, you can use the link in the email that arrives to verify that the share works as expected.

Presenting online

When you use the Present Online feature in PowerPoint 2013, you make your presentation available as a live presentation that others can view by using their web browsers. Your audience can follow as you lead the presentation process. Ideally, you would also be on a conference call (via the Lync application in Office or another service) to discuss the presentation while it appears on screen. You need to be signed in with your Microsoft account for the process to work via the free Office Presentation Service, and you need to have the presentation file open in PowerPoint. The process is simple and is an excellent way to give a live presentation to remote viewers.

Start and share the online presentation

1 On the ribbon, click the File tab to display the Backstage view.

2 Click the Share tab.

3 Click Present Online. Then, click the Present Online button that appears.

The Present Online dialog box informs you that it is preparing the online presentation.

(continued on next page)

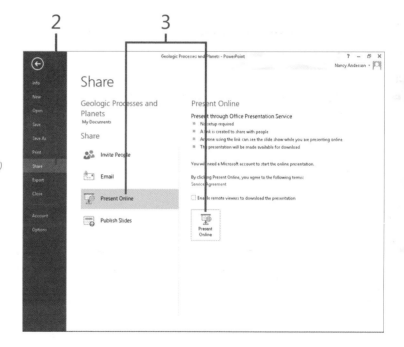

Start and share the online
presentation *(continued)*

4 Click Copy Link to copy the web address and then paste it into an email or IM message yourself (in Lync or another service). Or, click the Send In Email link to open an email message (usually in Outlook), enter the recipient email address information, and then send the email message to send the link.

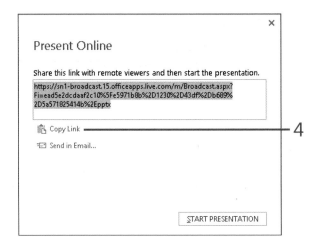

→ TRY THIS After you run the online presentation as described in the next task, use Copy Link and then paste the link into your web browser address bar and press Enter. Then, you can switch back and forth between PowerPoint and your web browser to practice running and viewing the show.

Run and close the online presentation

1 Follow the steps in the preceding task to set up the show and invite attendees. Then, click the Start Presentation button in the Present Online dialog box to begin the online presentation.

The slide show runs.

Use the navigational tools that appear when you hover the mouse pointer in the lower-left corner of the presentation screen.

2 Press Esc. Then, on the Present Online tab, in the Present Online group, click the End Online Presentation button to end the presentation.

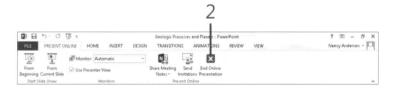

TIP All the tools that you can use to navigate or annotate a presentation are available to you when you are running an online presentation. For more about using them, see Section 14, "Running a presentation," starting on page 225.

Saving in other formats for sharing

You can use the Export options available in PowerPoint 2013 to save a presentation in a format that other users can view, even if they don't have PowerPoint. An easy format to use to share a presentation online is PDF (Portable Document Format). People with Adobe Acrobat or the free Adobe Reader can view the presentation just as they would the pages of a document. However, they cannot edit the file except to add comments or to highlight text.

You can save your PowerPoint presentation as a video that includes all the narration, timings, and animations you've built into it. People can then watch the video on their devices, or you might post it on the web on a video-sharing site such as YouTube.

Save a presentation as a PDF file

1 Click the File tab to display the Backstage view and then click the Export tab.

2 Click Create PDF/XPS Document. Then, click the Create PDF/XPS button that appears.

The Publish As PDF Or XPS dialog box opens.

(continued on next page)

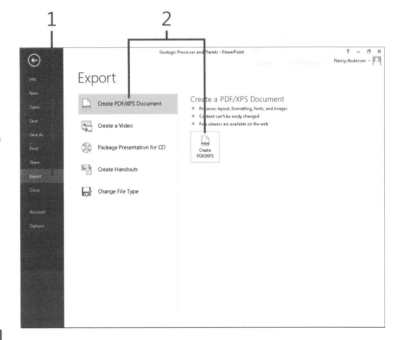

✓ TIP XPS is an electronic paper document technology developed by Microsoft that you can also use to share your presentation with others who don't have PowerPoint.

Save a presentation as a PDF file *(continued)*

3 Type a name for the document of up to 255 characters. You cannot use the characters * : < > | " \ or /.

4 Ensure that the Save As Type list shows the PDF format and then click Publish.

Assuming you left the Open File After Publishing check box checked as it is by default, the PDF document is displayed in an Adobe Reader window in Windows 7 or in the Reader app in Windows 8.

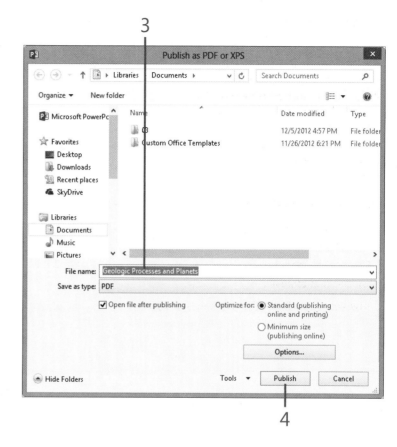

 TRY THIS To get a free copy of Adobe Reader, go to *http://get.adobe.com/reader/* and click the Download button.

 TIP If you click the File tab, click Share, and then click Email, you can click Send As PDF to send the current presentation file as an email message attachment in the PDF format.

Create a video

1 On the ribbon, click the File tab to display the Backstage view.

2 Click the Export tab.

3 Click Create A Video.

4 Click the first drop-down list and select the type of display that you want to use for the video presentation: Computer & HD Displays, Internet And DVD, or Portable Devices.

5 Click the next list and choose whether to use recorded timings and narrations with your video.

6 Use the Seconds Spent On Each Slide box to set the time each slide should be displayed in the video.

7 Click Create Video.

The Save As dialog box opens.

8 Enter another name in the File Name box, choose another save location if you want to, and then click Save. The video is saved to the specified folder. Go to the folder to view it.

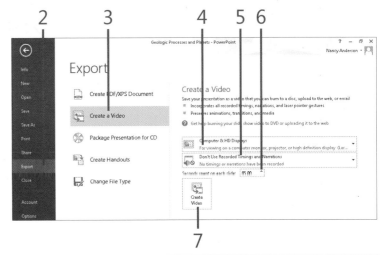

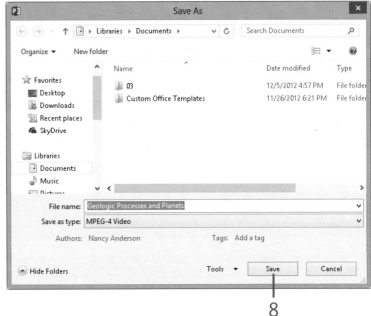

> ✓ **TIP** When you play a video file, if you haven't used preset timings, you can use the backward and forward arrows on your keyboard to move from slide to slide.

> ✓ **TIP** Saving a file as a video presentation can take a bit of time. Also, if you close PowerPoint before the video has been created, PowerPoint displays warning messages. It's a good idea to create a video when you have an errand to run or feel like multitasking with some other project.

Introducing advanced PowerPoint topics

17

The preceding sections of this book cover the topics you need in order to create most presentations and to use Microsoft PowerPoint 2013. However, the advanced features that you can explore in this section can help you to work more efficiently.

You can develop a presentation that forms the basis of other presentations and save that presentation as a template. This step can save you a great deal of work setting up backgrounds, layouts, and slide master settings for each new presentation.

Custom shows are subsets of the slides in a presentation that can be saved right inside the same file. Custom shows might contain only some of the slides in the presentation or rearrange the order of slides. For example, if you have a master presentation on your entire product line, you can save custom shows that focus on each product line separately and then show only the presentation that relates to an individual customer's needs.

You can use the Document Inspector to search for hidden data and remove it. You can add a digital signature that lets others who open the presentation that it came from you. Finally, you can customize the ribbon so it contains the tools you use most often.

Saving your own PowerPoint templates

You can save any file in a template format (.potx). A template can contain various custom settings, such as changes you make to the slide master, custom layouts or animations you created, or themes and font choices you applied. Your templates can also contain text or graphic elements in placeholders or on the slide master. By using a template as the basis of a new presentation, you not only save time but guarantee a consistency of look and feel among all your presentations.

Save a presentation as a template

1 Change any settings or make desired formatting changes to the presentation. Then, click the File tab to display the Backstage view.

2 Click the Export tab.

3 Click Change File type.

4 In the Change File Type list at the right, click Template.

5 Scroll down, if needed, and then click Save As.

The Save As dialog box opens.

(continued on next page)

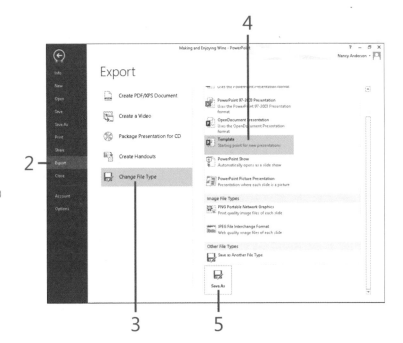

> **TIP**   If you have access to a Microsoft SharePoint site (either stand-alone or via Office 365) or a company intranet, you might consider sharing templates across an organization so that all presentations have a consistent company look and feel. You also can save and share a presentation from your SkyDrive, as described in "Saving a presentation to the cloud," on page 252.

Save a presentation as a template (continued)

6 In the File Name text box, enter a name for the template.

7 If it appears, you can double-click the Custom Office Templates folder to select it as the save location.

If Custom Office Templates doesn't appear or isn't the location where you want to save the template, click on the folder where you want to save the template in the Save As dialog box.

8 Click Save.

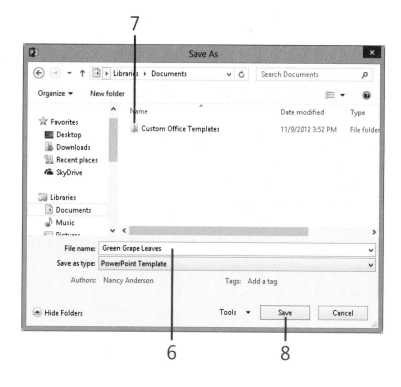

TIP If you or somebody else wants to use the template with an earlier version of PowerPoint, you should choose PowerPoint 97-2003 Template from the Save As Type list in the Save As dialog box. After you click Save, the Compatibility Checker will inform you of any features that will be removed when you save for the earlier version, Read the Summary and click Continue.

Use your template

1 Open a folder window from the Windows desktop and navigate to the folder that contains the template file.

2 Double-click the file.

A new presentation file based on the template opens in PowerPoint.

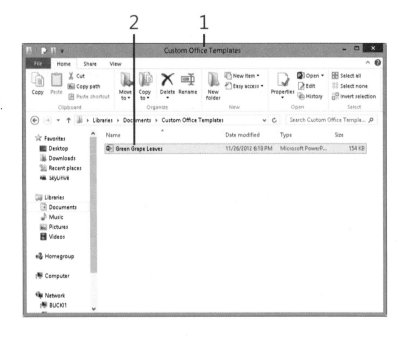

> **✓ TIP** Keep in mind that after you open a template, you need to save it as a regular PowerPoint presentation with a new name so that you don't overwrite the template with presentation-specific changes. For more information about saving files, see "Saving a PowerPoint presentation" on page 60 and "Closing a PowerPoint presentation" on page 63.

Creating custom shows

The ability to create and store custom shows within a single PowerPoint 2013 presentation file offers you great flexibility. You can create several custom shows from one presentation by simply choosing the slides to include and reorganizing them in any way you want. The slides in a custom show remain identical to the corresponding slides in your main presentation, but by selecting and rearranging their order, you can create quite different shows to meet the needs of your viewers.

Create a custom show

1 On the ribbon, click the Slide Show tab.

2 In the Start Slide Show group, click the Custom Slide Show button.

3 Click Custom Shows.

The Custom Shows dialog box opens.

4 Click New.

The Define Custom Show dialog box opens.

(continued on next page)

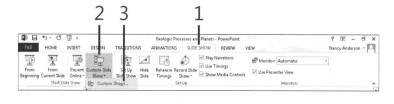

TIP If you change your mind about including a slide in a custom show, click that slide in the Slides In Custom Show list and then click the Remove button.

Create a custom show *(continued)*

5 Select the check box for a slide in the Slides In Presentation list.

6 Click Add. Repeat steps 5 and 6 to add all the slides that you want in your custom show.

7 Click a slide in the Slides In Custom Show list.

8 Use the Move Up and Move Down buttons to reorganize the slide order. Repeat this step with other slides until your slides are in the proper order.

9 In the Slide Show Name text box, enter a name.

10 Click OK.

11 Click Close to save your changes and dismiss the Custom Shows dialog box.

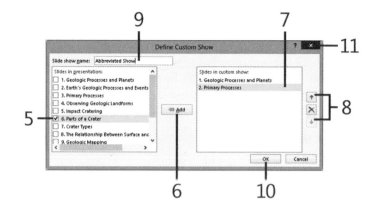

→ TRY THIS! If you created a custom show and need to edit it, click the Custom Slide Show button on the Slide Show tab. Select the show and then click the Edit button. Use the preceding steps to add, remove, or rearrange the slides in the show, and then click OK.

Run a custom show

1 On the ribbon, click the Slide Show tab.

2 In the Start Slide Show group, click the Custom Slide Show button.

3 Click the name of the custom show.

The show begins to run.

4 Use the navigation tools to move through the presentation. Press Esc to stop the show at any time.

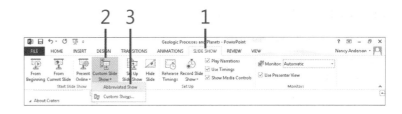

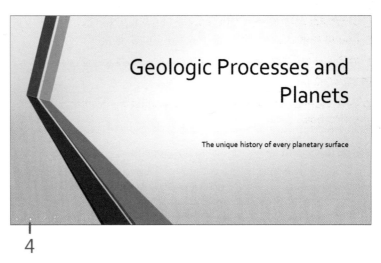

 TIP You can use the Set Up Show dialog box (click the Set Up Slide Show button on the Slide Show tab) to set up your file to play a custom show whenever you click the Slide Show button. Just select the custom show that you want to use from the Custom Show list.

SEE ALSO For more information about using navigation tools in Slide Show view, see "Navigating in a slide show" on page 230.

Removing hidden data by using the Document Inspector

When you intend to share a presentation, either by publishing it online or by handing it to somebody on a CD, it's a good idea to ensure that there isn't any hidden data included. For example, a file might contain personal information about the author or document properties (called *metadata*) that you'd rather not share. You can use the Document Inspector feature in Power-Point 2013 to remove such information.

Remove hidden data

1 Save a copy of your presentation with a new name.

2 On the ribbon, click the File tab to display the Backstage view.

3 Click the Info tab if it's not already selected.

4 In the Info section, click the Check For Issues button.

5 In the drop-down list that appears, click Inspect Document.

The Document Inspector dialog box appears.

(continued on next page)

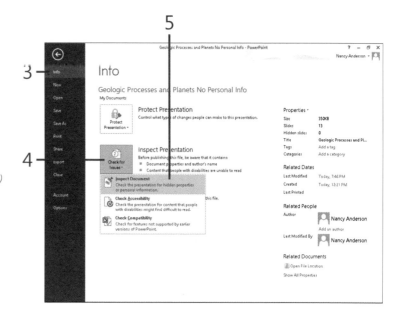

✓ **TIP** You started this task by saving a copy of the presentation because much of the data you delete using Document Inspector cannot be restored. If you don't save the file first, a window appears alerting you to this issue. The data that the Document Inspector removes might be useful information for a presentation you are still working on, such as the date you last made a change to the presentation or invisible contents on slides. Working on a copy preserves that data in the original.

Remove hidden data (continued)

6 Select the various check boxes to choose what content to check for.

7 Click Inspect.

8 Click any Remove All buttons that appear in the results window.

9 Click Close to save the file with the selected data omitted.

6 ———

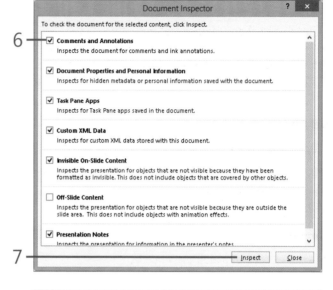

7 ———

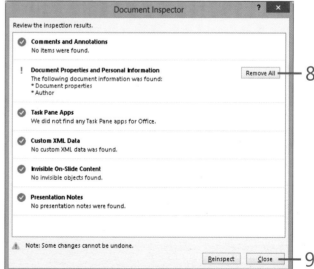

8

9

TRY THIS! If you want to manually edit your presentation properties to remove personal information instead of letting Document Inspector do all the work, on the ribbon, click the File tab, choose Info, and then click the Show All Properties link at the lower right. Delete any data in any field that you don't want included with the file.

Purchasing and using a digital signature

A digital signature is much like a handwritten signature on a check or other legal document. It can be used to ensure that the document was created by a particular person. In a world where computer files can contain potentially harmful materials, a digital signature helps to reassure recipients that a file was created by someone who know and trust. You can use a digital signature provided by a third party, which others can use to verify your document.

Buy and use a third-party digital signature product

1 Verify that your computer is connected to the Internet. Then, click the File tab to display the Backstage view.

2 On the Info tab, click the Protect Presentation button.

3 In the drop-down list that appears, click Add A Digital Signature.

4 In the confirming message pop-up box, click Yes.

Your computer's web browser launches and displays a webpage with the list of partner digital signing providers.

(continued on next page)

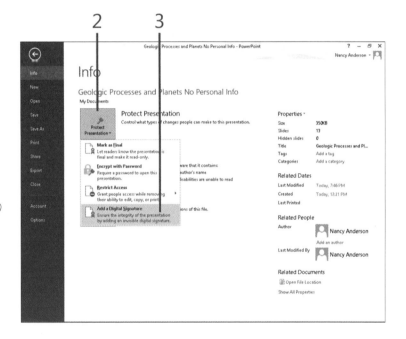

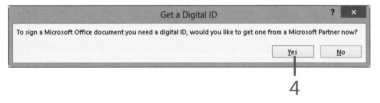

> **TIP** Digital signing software can cost anywhere from under $100 to over $250. You might make this investment if it's important that you ensure documents come from the person from whom they purport to be and that the contents of the document haven't been changed since they were signed.

Buy and use a third-party digital signature product *(continued)*

5 Select a digital signing provider in the list (which might change from time to time).

6 Use the prompts on the screen that appears and follow the steps to purchase a digital signature product or download a free trial.

These steps might vary slightly from service to service.

5

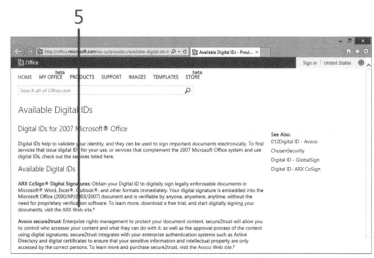

6

TRY THIS! You can also use the Information Rights Management Service to authenticate the sender and recipient of files sent by email to ensure that your files don't fall into the wrong hands. To do so, click the File tab and choose Info. Then, click the Protect Presentation button, choose Restrict Access, and then choose Connect To Digital Rights Management Servers And Get Templates. Follow the instructions to sign up for this service from Microsoft.

Customizing the ribbon

The idea behind the interface that started in Microsoft Office 2007 is that the most commonly used tools are present on the ribbon rather than buried in countless dialog boxes, and the tools you use less often, although accessible, aren't part of the main interface by default. Sometimes, the only way to access a function you might have used in a previous version of PowerPoint 2013 is to place a command on the ribbon.

Add buttons to the ribbon

1 On the ribbon, click the File tab to display the Backstage view and then click the Options tab.

The PowerPoint Options dialog box opens.

(continued on next page)

Info

New

Open

Save

Save As

Print

Share

Export

Close

Account

1— Options

> ⚠ **CAUTION**   Although you can add many tools to the ribbon, don't overdo it. Only add the tools you use most often, or add a tool to use a particular function and then remove it to clear clutter from the ribbon.

Add buttons to the ribbon (continued)

2 Click Customize Ribbon.

3 Under the Customize the Ribbon category on the right side, make sure that Main Tabs is selected, and then click New Tab or New Group. Use the Rename button to rename the tab or group.

4 Click the down-arrow on the Choose Commands From list, and select a category of tool, or simply scroll down and choose the Commands Not In The Ribbon category.

5 In the list on the left, click a command. Then, click the Add button to add it to the selected tab and group. Repeat this step for all of the tools that you want to add.

6 Click OK.

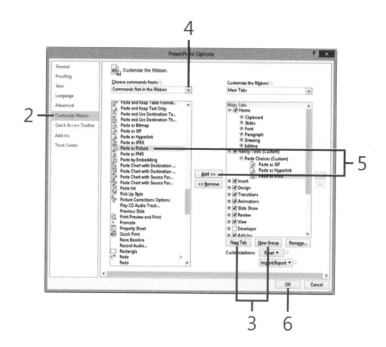

The new ribbon tab and its tools

✓ **TIP** If you change the ribbon and then want to revert to how it was when you installed PowerPoint, go to the PowerPoint Options dialog box, select Customize Ribbon, and then click Reset. The default ribbon settings are restored.

Remove or rearrange tools

1 On the ribbon, click the File tab to display the Backstage view and then click the Options tab.

The PowerPoint Options dialog box opens

2 Click Customize Ribbon.

3 In the Main Tabs list on the right, click a tab or group, Click the plus beside it to display its tools.

4 To remove it from the ribbon, click Remove,

5 To rearrange the tools, click Move Up or Move Down.

6 To save your settings, Click OK.

> **TIP** Be cautious about making changes to the ribbon because it might confuse others who use your copy of PowerPoint or even confuse you because the items on the ribbon will no longer match those in the Help system or books such as this one that you use to learn PowerPoint. You can use the Reset button on the Customize Ribbon tab of the PowerPoint Options dialog box to undo changes to the ribbon and Quick Access Toolbar.

Index

S

Save As dialog box, 30, 60–61, 252, 260
Save As screen, 30, 252
Save command, on Quick Access toolbar, 40
saving
    annotations, 59, 234, 235
    presentations, 60–62
        in other file formats, 258–259
        to cloud, 252–253
        to SkyDrive, 30, 62
        to USB drive or CD/DVD, 222–223
        as video, 260
    rehearsal timings, 221
    templates, 262–264
    timings for narrations, 219
scaling slide content, to new slide size, 125
screen layout for PowerPoint 2013, 9
ScreenTips
    displaying, 14
    for tools on ribbon, 37
scroll bar, in Thumbnails pane, 108
Search charm, 10
Search, for Help, 45
Search Online Templates And Themes text
    box, 49
Section Header layout, 82
sections, 107, 114–115
    renaming or deleting, 115
    summary slides for large presentation, 227
security, for shared presentations, 31
selecting
    multiple shapes, 29
    placeholders, 93–94
Selection pane, 93, 94
self-running, full-screen presentation, 215
Send Backward command, 184
sending slide shows by email, 213, 224
Send To Back command, 93, 184

<Separator> item, on Quick Access
    toolbar, 41
Set As Default Printer option, 246
settings, 36. *See also* PowerPoint Options
    dialog box
Set Up Show dialog box, 215, 216, 267
    Advance Slides section, 218
    Show Slides section, 217
shadow
    adding to object, 175
    for text, 170
Shape Fill gallery, 171
shapes
    applying effect, 174–175
    merging, 29
    outlines of, 173–174
    selecting multiple, 29
Shapes button, 38
Shapes gallery, 15, 161
sharing
    images on SkyDrive, 145
    presentations, 7, 251–260
        as email attachment, 259
        saving in other file formats for, 258–259
        from SkyDrive, 31, 254
    presentation template, 262
shortcut menus, 2
shortcuts. *See also* keyboard shortcuts
    for launching PowerPoint, 10
Show Presenter View option, 218
Show Without Animation option, 216
Show Without Narration option, 216
size changes
    for text, 167
    handles for, 176
    panes in Normal view, 55–56
    for pictures, 154
    for slides, 125
    for WordArt, 146

size of text, in Outline pane or Slide pane, 99
SkyDrive, 30, 52
    inserting pictures from, 144–145
    saving to, 62, 252–253
    sharing images on, 145
    sharing presentations from, 31, 254
slash, gray, as hidden slide marker, 112
Slide gesture, 7, 13
slide layouts
    Comparison, 129
    defined by themes, 66
    deleting, 74
    renaming, 73
slide masters, 65–80
    background, 72
    basics, 66
    deleting, 76
    displaying and navigating, 67
    graphics
        changing, 70–71
        overlapping other slide content, 71
    inserting, 75
    making changes, 68–69
Slide Master tab on ribbon
    Edit Master group, 66
        Delete, 74
        Insert Layout, 69
        Insert Slide Master, 75
        Rename, 73
    Edit Theme tools, 66
    Master Layout button, 69
Slide Master tools, 3
Slide Master view, 66, 67, 70–71
    adding layouts, 69
    applying custom animation in, 200
    closing, 67
    Thumbnails pane, 72, 73
Slide Navigator, 228
Slide pane, 55, 108

Z

zoom
    to part of slide, 228
    text in Outline pane, 98
    to page, in Print Preview, 245
    to part of slide, 229
Zoom slider
    for Slide Master view, 67
    for Slide pane contents, 108
    for slide preview, 55
    for Slide Sorter view, 57

About the Author

Nancy Muir is the author of more than 100 books on technology topics ranging from Windows and Office to nanotechnology and Internet safety. She runs a website, *TechSmartSenior.com*, that provides information about computers and the Internet for seniors, as well as writing a column on computers for *Retirenet.com*. Prior to her writing career, Nancy worked in computer book publishing and as a software training manager at Symantec Corporation. Nancy holds a certificate in distance learning design from the University of Washington and has taught technical writing and online safety at the university level.

What do you think of this book?

We want to hear from you!

To participate in a brief online survey, please visit:

microsoft.com/learning/booksurvey

Tell us how well this book meets your needs—what works effectively, and what we can do better.
Your feedback will help us continually improve our books and learning resources for you.

Thank you in advance for your input!

Microsoft®
Press

31901051954586